SMOKING
the inside story

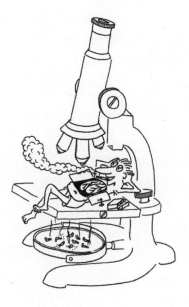

Dr Alex Milne is married with two children
who are approaching the age when they will be under
pressure to smoke.

After graduating in Electronic Engineering Science at the
University College of North Wales, Bangor, she researched
into the electrical activity of nerve cells, obtaining a PhD
in 1978 from University College London.

She continued working in neurophysiology and physiology,
including fetal respiratory physiology (University of Bristol)
and mechanisms of memory (University of Cambridge).

This book is dedicated to the memories of two friends,
Andy Le Page and Kathryn (Pip) Rowe,
whose specialist contributions and enthusiasm for the
whole venture are greatly valued.

SMOKING
the inside story

Alex Milne

with illustrations by James Northfield

Woodside
Communications

Published by Woodside Communications
High Onn, Church Eaton, Stafford ST20 0AX

First Published 1998

Alex Milne is hereby identified as author of this work
in accordance with Section 77 of the
Copyright, Designs and Patents Act 1988

ISBN 0 9533945 0 6

Designed and produced by Viners Wood Associates – 01452 812813.
Printed and bound in England by Biddles Limited.

Contents

Chapter 1   Tobacco and tobacco products   1

Chapter 2   Tobacco and money   15

Chapter 3   Tobacco smoke   24

Chapter 4   Where does the smoke go?   36

Chapter 5   Lungs, airways and bloodstream   39

Chapter 6   Other parts of the body   56

Chapter 7   Health professionals   67

Chapter 8   Passive smoking   74

Chapter 9   Old and young, quitting and smoking   85

Chapter 10   Rescue therapy   99

Chapter 11   Tales of smoking and quitting   110

Appendix I   The respiratory and circulatory systems in
             greater detail   123

Appendix II Glossary   155

Appendix III References   158

Index   165

Introduction

There is a huge amount of information on the effects of smoking, of great relevance to smokers, passive smokers and those who are tempted to smoke. However, much of this information is hidden away in the scientific and medical literature.

The aim of this book is to put current knowledge about smoking, snuff taking and tobacco chewing within reach of the non-specialist. It covers many aspects of tobacco, from its history and finance to what to do if you can't quit, but the core of the book deals with what happens when smoke gets inside the body. As well as information on smoking, the book presents the current state of knowledge on passive smoking, extending from adults spending the odd hour in smoky pubs to effects of smoking on the unborn, and even the unconceived, child.

The book is intended for anyone, including teenagers, who uses tobacco or who is wondering about it, as well as for those involved in advising others: parents, teachers and health professionals. It therefore includes some background information for those readers who have never studied the workings of the human body, and Appendix I treats the effects of smoke on the human body in greater detail.

In particular, the book shows the immediate damage caused to lungs, heart, blood vessels and blood by each puff of smoke as it arrives in the body. It also shows how this damage can progress to overt disease, sometimes years later. Few youngsters, puffing on their clandestine cigarettes, realize any harm is actually being done as they smoke. Most people in their teenage years feel immortal and are not impressed by the probability of illness 30 years hence; 30 years is an impossibly long time off.

What all smokers, passive smokers and potential smokers ought to know about, and no-one so far seems to have pointed out, is the damage to body tissues with every drag inhaled. This book sets out to fill that gap.

Whose decision?

Sooner or later, most people get offered a cigarette. For many, it happens when they are young and much of their knowledge about smoking comes from tobacco company publicity and from their social set.

Most youngsters who experiment with smoking believe that they won't actually get hooked themselves. With no first-hand experience of addiction this is only natural, but very few indeed escape addiction. After the second or third cigarette, it is probably too late.

Taking up smoking is a huge decision, one which could well be with the smoker till they die and which will cost a great deal of money: £1000 a year for the average habit in late 1990s Britain.

If you have children, make sure they know all about smoking, particularly the bits the tobacco ads leave out. Start talking to them well before the age when they might begin smoking. If 6-year-olds can recognise tobacco brand names on racing cars, they can start to discuss the reasons why those brand names are there.

If you don't smoke but are feeling tempted or pressurized to start, take your decision on the basis of all the facts. Above all else, make sure it is your decision, not someone else's.

Acknowledgements

I am grateful to many friends and colleagues for their help and criticism in the preparation of this book. In particular, I should like to thank Professor Robert West and Drs Lynn Bindman, Elizabeth Y Davis, Jane Houchin and Jenny Jessop for helpful discussions and for reviewing the final draft. Thanks also to Professor Gareth Jones, Drs Peter Bregestovski, Charles Buckley, Chris Jones and the late Andy Le Page BDS, LDS, RCS (Eng), and Messrs Stephen Clayton, Etienne Duke BDS, Andy Joynt and Roger Milne for their specialist contributions, and also to Dr Jim Cooper, Charlotte Hammersley and Jim and Ruth Milne for their very valuable comments as non-specialist readers. Thanks also to all the smokers, ex-smokers and never smokers who agreed to be interviewed.

I should also like to thank ASH for their help and information, and the Sunday Times for permission to quote from 'Come to Cancer Country – Who's Lucky Now' by Janine di Giovanni. © Times Newspapers Limited, 1992.

The author can be contacted via smoking@woodside.globalnet.co.uk

Sources of information on smoking and quitting.

ASH (Action on Smoking and Health) is a charity, founded in 1971 by the Royal College of Physicians. Send an A5-sized stamped addressed envelope to receive their catalogue of publications. These range from factsheets, kept up-to-date on all aspects of tobacco, to books, booklets, videos etc. giving detailed treatments of particular topics (e.g. tobacco advertising, passive smoking, advice to companies). A small selection of factsheets is free of charge.

ASH, 16, Fitzhardinge St, London W1H 9PL
Tel. 0171 224 0743

QUIT is an independent charity whose aim is 'helping smokers to quit'. They run a free telephone helpline, 1-9 pm weekdays, 1-5 pm weekends, and 9 am to 11 pm seven days a week during their campaign periods, for people who want to talk to someone about quitting. They will also send out free information packs. In addition, QUIT can offer advice to companies on introducing smoking policies at work.

QUIT, Victory House, 170 Tottenham Court Rd, London W1P 0HA
Tel. 0171 388 5775   Free Helpline 0800 00 22 00

There are local sources of advice listed in the phone book: the Health Education Authority, GP or pharmacist should be able to advise directly as well as provide information about any self-help or similar groups.

CHAPTER 1
Tobacco and tobacco products

Snorting snuff

The tobacco plant is a member of the nightshade family (*Solanaceae*), to which potatoes, tomatoes, aubergines and deadly nightshade also belong. A native of the Western Hemisphere, tobacco, like potatoes, spread to Europe after trade was established with the Americas in the 16th century, and thence swiftly to all parts of the world.

Today it is an important crop in more than 60 countries, with the largest producer by far being China. The annual worldwide production of tobacco in the early 1990s was about seven million tonnes, rising to eight million in the mid 1990s.

A superking cigarette, without its filter, weighs about 0.7 grams, so eight million tonnes of tobacco would make over 2,000 cigarettes each for the entire human race. In fact, about one third of the world's population over fifteen years old are smokers, and plenty below that age smoke too.

1

There are two commercially important species of tobacco, both of which were under cultivation by Native Americans when the Europeans arrived. *Nicotiana tabacum* was grown in the areas which are now the West Indies, South America and much of Mexico, while *Nicotiana rustica* was cultivated by most tribes east of the Mississippi River and also in what is now the Southwestern US and Northern Mexico.

Tobacco use in pre-European America

Christopher Columbus first landed on Hispaniola in the West Indies in November 1492. His men saw something unknown in Europe: the people of the island emitting smoke, which dragon-like feat they achieved by puffing on pipes or burning rolls of vegetation. It must have been an astonishing sight, but hardly more so than their snuff-taking, which involved poising one end of a Y-shaped hollow cane just above a pile of fine powder, inserting the other two ends into the nostrils and snorting up.

According to one report, the name these Carib people gave to their snuff-snorter was *tobago* or *tobaca* and the Spaniards took this name and gave it to the plant we now call tobacco. A competing claim is that *tobago* was the name of the pipe used, and a third that something similar was the name of the cigars they rolled. Perhaps the newcomers had missed the point and *tobago* was already the name of the plant they were snorting, chewing and smoking.

Dated historical records of the Native Americans are sparse compared with those for similar periods in Europe and Asia, but tobacco smoking originated at least as early as AD 100, when it is shown in use in religious ceremonies in Mayan art. The Mayan term for smoking, *sik'ar*, is almost certainly the origin of the Spanish word *cigarro*, from which cigar and subsequently cigarette have been derived. Northward movement of Mayans from their homelands in the Yucatan area of Central America spread the cultivation and use of tobacco.

As settlers from Europe advanced over the newly-discovered continent, which Columbus always believed was the Far East, they found tobacco in widespread use. When Cortes conquered the Aztecs in what is now Mexico, only 27 years after Columbus made landfall in the New World, he found them smoking hollow reeds stuffed with tobacco. In other parts of Central and South America the tobacco was wrapped in the outer leaves of maize (corn on the cob) or other vegetation for smoking.

In 1616 the French, in what is now Ontario, Canada, found an Iroquoian-speaking clan, the Tionontati, whose cultivation of tobacco was so extensive that they named them 'The Tobacco Nation'.

Amongst the native tribes of North America smoking had a strong ritual value in the peace pipe, and snuff-taking and chewing of the leaves were also common. Tobacco was held by them to be of medicinal value, a strong factor in its eager acceptance by European adventurers to the New World.

Tobacco imported to Europe

Although Columbus' attempts at establishing a Spanish colony in the West Indies were unsuccessful, others followed and in 1535 substantial tobacco plantations were laid out there. The Spaniards took seed as well as tobacco back to Spain and farmers there began to grow it. Until about 1575, the Spanish had a virtual monopoly on the small but growing commercial tobacco production for Europe. All imports were from the Orinoco region (now Venezuela) and the West Indies, both of which were under Spanish control.

Most European smoking, initially the preserve of the wealthy, was in pipes, with some cigars, but tobacco was also popular as snuff. Because of the belief in its medicinal powers, tobacco was even made into poultices. In 1560, the French ambassador to Portugal, Jean Nicot, sent some snuff to Paris for the French Queen Catherine of the Medicis. She was delighted with it; it became fashionable at her court and Nicot gained the distinction of giving his name to both nicotine and the genus of tobacco, *Nicotiana*.

More than one account exists of the arrival in Europe of cigarettes. One version suggests that at the beginning of the 17th century, hand-rolled cigarettes were introduced into Europe by Spanish sailors. Another is far more colourful: at the beginning of the 16th century, beggars in the streets of Seville began picking up the discarded cigar butts of the wealthy and trendy. They broke them down and rolled the tobacco up in scraps of paper to smoke. These became known as *cigarillos* (little cigars). After a couple of hundred years, this style of smoking, though presumably not the source of the tobacco, gained respectability, but it was the French troops during the Napoleonic Wars who called them by the name which has stuck: cigarettes.

Importance to American settlers

Attempts by Europeans, mainly English, to settle on the mainland of North America, as the Spanish control of the West Indies seemed complete, had met with terrible hardship and failure. Sir Walter Raleigh had originally claimed land for his Queen, Elizabeth I, naming it 'Virginia' (which in those days included what is now North Carolina) in her honour and establishing a colony on Roanoke Island

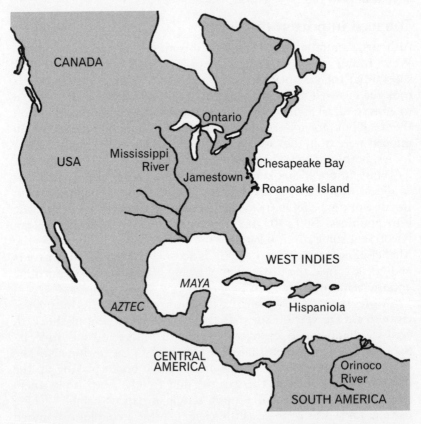

in 1585. It failed, as did a second two years later. Then in 1606, with James I of England and VI of Scotland on the throne, the Virginia Company was set up with the aim of forming a better funded and therefore more viable and ultimately profitable settlement. The new site on Chesapeake Bay, to the north of Raleigh's old colonies, was named Jamestown in honour of the King, and the settlers arrived in

1607. They, too, struggled and suffered. Half of them died in the first winter but the survivors clung on and gained an increasing foothold on the new continent.

Things remained very hard until 1612, when the English settler John Rolfe, whose marriage to Pocahontas, daughter of a local Chief, had caused a stir back in London, began commercial tobacco cultivation with seeds of *N. tabacum* from the Orinoco region of South America. The climate and soil were ideal for the newly introduced seeds, which thrived.

Even before the Virginia plantations, tobacco had spread to Germany, Russia, Turkey, Persia, West Africa, the Philippines, Japan and China, so demand was strong and rising. With an existing market and the means of supplying it, the fortunes of the new colony were assured and the foundations of the American tobacco industry were laid.

In the short term, the commercial success of the Jamestown plantations turned a struggling settlement into a viable and thriving community, attracting increasing numbers of people from Britain. Within a decade, the profits from tobacco were so great that restrictions had to be placed on tobacco planting to allow food crops to be grown; starvation was a real possibility. Tobacco was the main export by a large margin and paid for plentiful imports of all kinds of goods. Wages and even taxes were paid in tobacco and for a while it was equivalent to currency.

The commercial success of this enterprise, coupled with political factors and religious persecution in Britain (around the time of the Civil War) and Europe, inclined large numbers of people to search for a new life in the new and promising colonies under the control of the British Crown. The development of modern America was under way and the success of the British Colonies, initially founded on tobacco, made them the core of the USA (Washington DC is not far from Jamestown) and English its predominant language.

Smoke, money and monarchs

The most famous tobacco anecdote from Britain belongs to Queen Elizabeth I and her then favourite, Sir Walter Raleigh. A dashing, handsome and ambitious Captain of the Guard and seafaring adventurer, he had eagerly taken up the new habit of pipe smoking, which intrigued the Queen. He bet that he could weigh the smoke generated by the pipe in his mouth; the bet was accepted and he proceeded to weigh the pipe, smoke it and weigh it again, when it was considerably lighter. The Queen is said to have remarked with delight that plenty of men turned money into smoke but only Walter could turn smoke into money.

Despite Raleigh's reputation for having introduced smoking to England, his influence was in popularizing it. It was Sir John Hawkins who in 1565 first brought tobacco from Florida, and Sir Richard Greville in 1585 (the year of Raleigh's first attempted colony) and Captain John Lane a year later who brought pipes and tobacco, and thus provided Raleigh with the materials for his wager.

Not all rulers were so pleased with the new fashion. Elizabeth's successor James I of England and VI of Scotland, in whose honour Jamestown was named, hated it so much that not only did he forbid its production in Britain and impose punitive taxes in order (unsuccessfully) to discourage its use, he published in 1604 'A Counterblast to Tobacco'. In it, he described smoking as:

> 'A branch of the sin of drunkenness, which is the root of all sins.'
>
> 'A custom loathsome to the eye, hateful to the nose, harmful to the brain, dangerous to the lungs, and in the black, stinking fume thereof, nearest resembling the horrible Stygian smoke of the pit that is bottomless.'
>
> 'Herein is not only a great vanity, but a great contempt of God's good gifts, that the sweetness of man's breath, being a good gift of God, should be willfully corrupted by this stinking smoke.'

He was not the only leader to try to ban tobacco. In Russia and Turkey, severe penalties were incurred by its users. In America, the Puritans condemned it as a dangerous narcotic, and as late as the end of the 19th century there was a Royal Edict banning it in Abyssinia. Some religions still ban the use of tobacco and many disapprove.

Cultivation and harvesting

These days, *N. tabacum* is the main cultivated species of tobacco worldwide and the only species commercially produced in the US, but *N. rustica*, the species of the 'Oriental tobaccos', is an important crop in the former USSR, Turkey and India as well as some parts of Europe.

N. tabacum is an annual, which is to say that it grows freshly from seed each year. The seeds themselves are tiny. A healthy plant can produce a million seeds, but their small size makes them unsuitable for planting directly in the ground. They are sprinkled onto soil in cold frames and tamped in. Within 10 weeks they are big

Nicotiana tabacum

enough to plant out and in a further 10-13 weeks the leaves are ready for harvesting. As soon as the cluster of flowers, small, pink and trumpet-shaped, begins to develop at the top of the plant, it is cut off to encourage leaf growth. The final height varies according to the variety grown, the soil, the climate and any added fertilizers; the smallest are little over waist height and the tallest could hide a horse.

N. rustica tends to be smaller and its flowers are yellow. It has more perennial tendencies than *N. tabacum* but commercially is generally treated as an annual.

In the US, planting, as well as some harvesting, tends to be done by machine but, even there, tobacco is a labour-intensive crop, requiring 300 work-hours per acre (740 per hectare). In less developed countries the work is done by hand. Wherever it is grown, it provides employment for many people as well as a handsome return for the grower.

Each plant bears about 20 leaves. The leaves are large, at least as long as an arm and slightly over half as wide as they are long. They are ready for harvesting when they begin to change colour, becoming a lighter shade of green and rather mottled. Harvesting is done either by cutting individual leaves as they ripen ('priming') or by cutting the whole plant. In either case, they are then cured, the first step in the process of producing a saleable tobacco product.

Curing and marketing

Curing is all about improving the flavour and burning quality. Fresh tobacco tastes sharp and bitter, but careful curing results in the products that are so irresistible to millions the world over. The curing process involves a host of chemical reactions within the leaves, with a little fermentation and partial decomposition under the influence of the resident bugs as well as considerable drying.

7

There are three main ways of curing tobacco: air curing, fire curing and flue or bulk curing, and each lends itself to different varieties of tobacco plant.

Air curing

All curing was originally done by hanging the leaves up to dry naturally in the air. Air curing, in well-ventilated barns, is still done in many places and used for specific products in the US but can take four to eight weeks, depending on the weather. In some places, or for specific products, tobacco is cured directly in the sun.

Fire curing

The next development was fire curing. Hardwood fires (softwoods, e.g. pine or spruce, contain pitch and their smoke would impart a bitter flavour and tacky black covering to the leaves) are lit on the floor of the barn, the heat speeding up the process, although care must be taken not to scorch the leaves. Fire curing can be done in three days, or can take six weeks, but it takes skill to achieve consistent quality and the end product is distinctive.

Fire curing was originally developed to process the tobacco sufficiently to allow it to survive the long sea voyages to Europe and beyond, but the smoke imparts a flavour to the tobacco. In and around Virginia in the early 19th century, charcoal, which produces far less smoke for the heat it puts out, began to be used instead. Some specialist tobaccos are fire cured with particular wood smoke to achieve a particular flavour, just as for example hickory may be preferred over oak for smoking meat or fish.

Flue and bulk curing

Nowadays, the majority of US cigarette tobacco is flue-cured, i.e. hung in closed barns which are heated, originally by flues from exterior fires. More modern methods use heated pipes or oil or gas burners. The temperature is gradually raised to about 70° C, drying the leaves progressively. This can bring the curing time down to as little as three days, is highly controllable and so produces a consistent quality with low labour costs – an obvious economic gain. Care has to be taken that the air in the curing barn is neither too hot nor too moist and that the leaves are not touching each other. Individual leaves are strung on wires or spikes and whole plants are hung on 'tobacco sticks' which then slot into racks.

Bulk curing is a modern development of flue curing, where hot air is forced through loosely packed leaves between metal racks in highly specialized barns.

In the US, flue or bulk cured tobacco is the main component of cigarettes and 95% of this type of tobacco goes to the cigarette industry. This is the stuff known the world over as 'Virginia'.

Geographically, tobacco varieties suitable for flue or bulk curing are grown down the East Coastal plain, to the east of the Appalachian mountains and down to Florida. Tobacco varieties for fire curing, the smallest volume tobacco product in the US, tend to be grown further west, in West Virginia, Kentucky and Tennessee. They have broad, very dark green and slightly tacky leaves, and their main use is in snuff. The remainder of US-grown tobacco is air cured and goes largely for cigars, though some is blended into cigarettes.

Sorting and ageing

The next process is to remove the leaf from the stems if plants have been cut and cured whole. It involves putting some moisture back into the leaves to prevent cracking. Methods vary from steam to storage in damp cellars. The separate leaves are then sorted into bundles according to their colour, size and quality; these bundles are known as hands. The hands are packed into barrels (called hogsheads), bales or casks, at which point they are ready for sale. Some leaf is sold directly from the farm, especially the high-quality cigar tobacco leaf, but the bulk goes to market, generally to auction.

After purchase, the tobacco moisture content is adjusted to 10%, which generally means drying. The exact moisture content is critical; too dry and the leaves shatter, too damp and they go mouldy. The tobacco is then repacked and left to age for one to three years in containers, during which time a considerable amount of fermentation takes place. The result is a much sweeter and milder taste, and a lower nicotine content.

Price support

Such is the nature of agriculture now that many governments have price support systems for produce, and tobacco is no exception. It is a huge earner, both directly and as a tax-raiser, and it is in the interests of all financially involved to cushion the producers through poor seasons or poor market conditions. A price support mechanism guarantees a minimum price to the producer, and this is generally achieved by co-operatives or government agencies buying up surplus and storing it until it can be sold on.

Notwithstanding this, tobacco is a cash crop of significant profitability. In, for example, the US, many growers claim that there is no alternative crop offering a comparable return.

Cigarettes

Cigarettes were the last form of smoking to be devised and now account for the overwhelming bulk of tobacco consumption. They have come a long way since the days of the beggars of Seville.

When cigarettes were first made commercially they were hand rolled on a table, the paper was pasted and closed by hand and they were hand packed. In 1880, an American, James Bonsack, was granted a patent for a machine which fed the shredded tobacco into a long strip of paper which it rolled round the tobacco and sealed, effectively making an endless cigarette. This was cut into individual cigarettes as it emerged. Three years later the machine was imported into England, and over the following few years the cigarette making industry spread throughout Europe.

The big factor in increasing the popularity of cigarettes came in the first half of the 20th century. Changes in the cultivation of tobacco and in the processing resulted in a milder smoke, which made it easier to inhale than any previous smoking mixture.

From the fermented leaf, the process is roughly as follows. The midribs and veins are removed from the leaf (if this has not been done earlier), which is then cut into strips. At this stage, the blending of different tobacco types takes place. Tastes vary around the globe but seem consistent within national boundaries. Next, various additives, some of them secret, go in. These may be things like glycerine or apple juice, which help retain moisture, or flavourings such as liquorice, mint or sugar. Cigarette manufacturers are understandably reluctant to divulge exactly what goes in with the tobacco. Tight restrictions on cigarette additives are in force in the UK, more so than in most other countries.

Virginia (flue cured, also known as Bright because of its bright yellowish colour after curing) is the major component of cigarettes. Taste in the UK is for Virginia alone, although different qualities and years' production will be blended to achieve consistency from year to year.

Additives, some of them secret

In the US, a tobacco called Burley or White Burley is blended in. This is a variety derived from a few light-coloured plants noticed by an Ohio tobacco farmer in 1864 and is now extensively cultivated. It is air cured, very light in colour and is porous and absorptive. It is also higher in nicotine (3.5–4%) than Virginia, which is 2.5–3% nicotine. US blends also contain up to 10% imported Oriental tobacco, mainly from Turkey but also from Greece and nearby countries, which is the smaller *N. rustica*. It is aromatic but relatively low (less than 2%) in nicotine, despite the fact that, prior to curing, *N. rustica* is higher in nicotine than is *N. tabacum*. Oriental tobacco is air cured in the sun, and sunlight breaks down nicotine.

Other countries prefer other balances of tobaccos and flavours, and most producer countries lean heavily towards locally-produced tobacco. China, by far the world's largest grower, produces almost entirely for home consumption, as do India and the countries of the former USSR.

The tobacco blend and additives are tumbled in drums to mix them thoroughly, then shredded finely into 'rag', the familiar contents of the cigarette. Modern machines can turn out thousands of cigarettes a minute as well as sticking filters on the end. The filters are made of cellulose acetate. They trap some of the tar, nicotine and particles from the inhaled smoke and also cool it slightly, making it easier to inhale.

Cigars

Cigars use three kinds of leaf, all of the darker kinds of tobacco and all air cured. The majority, about 80%, is called filler and is cut leaf. It is chosen for its sweet flavour and even burning qualities. It is packed inside a binder, which in the very best cigars is a certain kind of leaf but is now commonly binder sheet, a kind of paper made from reconstituted coarse or damaged leaves. The whole is then wrapped spirally in a wrapper leaf. These, the most expensive leaf in the cigar, have to be strong, thin, elastic and of a silky texture; they are grown under a cloth-covered frame, which makes them highly labour-intensive. Reconstituted tobacco sheet is widely used now instead of wrapper leaf, though less so than binder sheet. The most expensive cigars are, of course, still traditionally bound and wrapped.

The spiral wrapping is begun at the end to be lit, so that the wrapper doesn't unwind when its fastening goes up in smoke. Lighting the wrong end of a cigar is a spectacularly visible social crime.

The finest cigar wrapper leaf in the world is produced in a small area on the coast of Sumatra, Indonesia. Cuba shares with Java the distinction of producing the best cigar filler. Most cigar leaf is grown fairly close to the equator, although a certain amount is grown in parts of the USA.

Smoking tobacco

This is the name given to pipe and hand-rolling cigarette tobacco. Blends vary enormously but tend to contain more dark coloured tobaccos than do cigarettes. It is generally a blend of Burley, flue cured and dark air cured tobaccos with any of a huge range of additives and flavourings.

Its smoke, along with that from cigars, is more alkaline than cigarette smoke. This favours nicotine absorption from the mouth rather than lungs and also makes it harder to inhale. Because the smoke is not inhaled to any great extent, nicotine uptake is less and slower, which means less addiction and a lower risk of lung cancer. However, it does cause more mouth cancer. Although the overall health risk from

Lighting the wrong end of the cigar . . .

pipe and cigar smoking (as long as it is non-inhaling) is lower than from cigarette smoking, it is still higher than for not smoking.

Chewing tobacco

Chewing was commonplace before the Europeans arrived in the New World and in the 19th century it became a highly distinctive American habit. This may have been because it was easier for people on the move to obtain their nicotine without having to light up, but it was also partly a post-independence reaction against European cigar and pipe smoking. An essential part of tobacco chewing is spitting (for those who don't care to swallow the juice), which is fine in the saddle but accounts for the spittoons in American bar rooms and the sawdust on the floors. Tobacco chewing was also commonplace in rural parts of the UK until the second world war, when cigarettes, issued to service people, really took over.

An 1860 census for Virginia and North Carolina recorded 348 tobacco factories. Of these, 335 produced nothing but chewing tobacco and a further six only produced pipe tobacco as a sideline, using up the scrap from the chewing tobacco.

There were different kinds of chewing tobacco: Fine Cut, an expensive blend of finely shredded, uncompressed leaf; Navy, a cake of Burley, highly flavoured with liquorice, rum, spices, sugar, honey or a whole range of other substances; Flat Plug, a compressed cake of Bright tobacco, sometimes lightly sweetened; Twist, a coarse dark tobacco twisted into ropes; and Scrap, the trimmings and leaf ends left over from cigar making.

Tobacco chewing was also popular among sailors the world over, presumably because on board ship, especially in the days of sail, keeping smoking materials dry was difficult, fire was a deadly hazard but spitting (downwind) was no problem at all.

Chewing tobacco was largely abandoned when cigarettes became available and its use in industrialized countries is now very small. The social unacceptability of spitting as compared with tipping ash doubtless played a part, but in countries like India and Sri Lanka chewing is still common.

Snuff

The last of the tobacco products, snuff is the greatest user of fire cured leaf. It undergoes much longer fermentation than other tobaccos and is finely ground and flavoured with oils and spices. It became very stylish in Europe during the 17th century and worldwide from the 18th, and snuff boxes were highly ornamented fashion essentials for the very wealthy. Inhalation was the favoured method and was less frowned upon for women than was smoking. People used to grate their own snuff from cut leaf, carrying tiny graters with their snuff boxes for the purpose.

Snuff 'dipping', the other method of taking snuff, involves rubbing it on the gums or holding a wadge in the cheek, where it mixes with saliva and the nicotine can be absorbed. This is particularly popular in Sweden at present. A new kind of ground tobacco product in a 'tea bag' was launched in Britain some years ago. Designed to be held in the mouth and sucked, it was akin to snuff dipping but without the bits. Its logo 'Skoal Bandits' was to be seen on Formula 1 racing cars but it was banned in the UK in 1989. The ban was viewed by cynics as little more than a commercially inexpensive sop to the anti-tobacco lobby because, at the time, the market for the product was very small.

CHAPTER 2
Tobacco and money

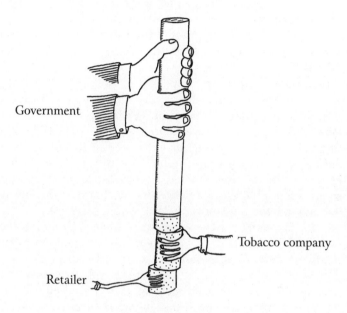

Government

Tobacco company

Retailer

Who gets what?

Anyone who smokes is only too well aware of the cost of a packet of cigarettes, but who gets what of that retail price in the UK?

The retail margin is about 7%, i.e. retailers keep about 7 pence from every pound paid over for cigarettes. They are also liable to a fine of up to £2,500, set to rise, if they get caught selling them to anyone under the age of 16. (The possibility of raising the age to 18 is under discussion.)

The Government levies three separate taxes: firstly, a tax which is a fixed amount per 1,000 cigarettes and is reviewed annually by the Chancellor of the Exchequer; secondly, an excise duty which is 20% of the retail price and thirdly, VAT at 17.5% on the price including the other taxes.

Taking a round figure of £3.00 for 20 cigarettes, total tax including VAT is about £2.38, though with tax on cigarettes being increased at more than the rate of inflation, as cigarettes get more expensive the proportion of their price which goes in tax is also rising.

With the retailer's margin at 21p, the remaining 41p pays for the tobacco, paper, filter, manufacturing, packaging, distribution and advertising, and tobacco companies still turn in a thundering profit.

Unlike retailers, the Government is not directly penalized for sales to children. It is estimated that in 1994, 11–15-year-olds smoked well over a billion cigarettes, from which the government netted £108 million in tax – more than ten times the £10 million they spent on anti-smoking campaigns.

The Government's total excise plus VAT income from smoking in 1994/95 was just short of £9 billion (£9,000 million). The NHS in England and Wales spent less than 7% of this (£610 million) on treating smokers for smoking-related diseases. Including things like invalidity benefit to people disabled by the diseases of smoking, losses arising from fires started by smoking materials, and the treatment of passive smoking diseases in children, the bill rises to £1,200 million for England and Wales. Even if we add a generous amount for Scotland, the Government is, financially and in the short term, laughing – but then, governments are constrained to think of the relatively short (5 year) term interests of the electorate.

After years of only voluntary agreements to control tobacco advertising, the Labour Government of 1997 promised to ban sports sponsorship by tobacco companies. Tobacco advertising can only be

A change of sponsors . . .

banned by the EC, though with the new support rather than the previous opposition of the UK Government, this is a real possibility. Many countries have already banned much tobacco promotion and the results in terms of smoking reduction, particularly among children, are encouraging.

The announcement that Formula 1 is to move away from tobacco sponsorship is welcome. Its use for advertising tobacco is effective, judged by reports that children who watch Formula 1 are twice as likely to smoke as those who don't. The sport claims not to be viable without sponsorship; given that each driver uses a new engine for each race and each practice day, the claim seems quite reasonable. As the Pacific Rim, a major target area for tobacco companies, provides 70% of the Formula 1 television audience, alternative sponsors will have to be interested in targeting this region. Spectator health and safety should benefit from the change.

Tobacco companies

Financial details from tobacco companies for 1993 are as follows.

Imperial Tobacco (John Player, Embassy, Regal), which is part of Hanson plc, had roughly 30% of the UK market in 1993, a turnover of £3,070 million and an operating profit of £308 million. (Operating profit is the money made on the operation of the business. It can differ from the pre-tax profit if, for example, the company has large investments earning interest, or debts, the interest on which can be deducted from the operating profit.)

Gallaher (Benson & Hedges, Silk Cut), owned by the US company American Brands, had roughly 50% of the UK market in 1993, with a turnover of £5,060 million and a pre-tax profit of £362 million. Only about 72% of Gallaher's 1992 sales were tobacco; they also have financial interests in the supply chain (Forbuoys, NSS newsagents) and completely outside tobacco [Dollond & Aitchison (optics), Whyte & Mackay (spirits)].

Rothmans, with 15% of the UK market, is a bit more complicated. It is UK based but owned by a Swiss company which, in turn, is owned by the South African based Rembrandt Corporation but it has acquired rights to sell Philip Morris brands (Marlboro, Raffles) in addition to its own Rothman's Royals, Dunhill, Consulate, Peter Stuyvesant and Black Cat. Its pre-tax profits were similar to those of Gallaher and Imperial (£340 million).

BAT Industries (formerly British American Tobacco), which is

UK-based, is in a different league; its pre-tax profits for 1993 were £1210 million from tobacco and £913 million from financial services (Eagle Star and Allied Dunbar). It produces 27 billion cigarettes a year in the UK (about 9 per day for every legitimate smoker in the country) but markets very few of them locally, most of its production going to Africa and the Far East. It owns, wholly or partly, tobacco companies in 45 countries around the world.

All these pre-tax profits attract corporation tax, which gives the Exchequer somewhere handy to another £1 billion (some of this comes from sales outside the UK) to add to the £9 billion in excise duty and VAT – a round sum of £10 billion a year, or getting on for £200 for every man, woman and child in the country.

Advertising

Since 1993, Imperial has picked up some market share at Gallaher's expense. Tobacco company executives are frequently challenged over the morality of recruiting new, especially under-age, smokers and they keep trotting out the argument that advertising is about persuading existing smokers to switch brands.

Doubtless competition between brands is very fierce, so the argument is not total rubbish, but their claim that advertising is only about switching brands, and not at all about increasing the market, is implausible. When a company already has 50% of the market share in any commodity, trying to increase that share has lower potential rewards than trying to expand the market. The head of a leading UK advertising agency, who surely knows his trade, described the tobacco companies' claim as 'so preposterous it is insulting'.

Advertising is more than a question of sticking up a few posters and hoping that sales will rise. Campaigns are carefully planned with specific aims and target groups. Their launch is often co-ordinated with high-profile sponsorship (for example snooker: billboard adverts for the sponsoring brand will go up to coincide with a televised event). Detailed studies are undertaken to assess the impact of the advertising and success can consist of increased sales of a few percent, sometimes even less. The effects of advertising, in all fields, are extremely closely studied. Whatever the tobacco companies would like us to believe, their campaigns are as closely thought out as any other.

They have an intrinsic problem: tobacco, despite being legally on sale, kills. In the UK alone, just to replace dead customers they need to recruit 300 new smokers a day.

In an amoral world, it would make sense to aim cigarette advertising at children on the grounds that they provide easier pickings than adults, and well over half of adult smokers started before they were 16. Naturally rebellious, children can be relied on to go against the advice of 'serious' people who lecture them on the dangers of smoking. To the young, life stretches infinitely ahead. They are immortal; nothing can get them; 30 years hence is impossibly far away, so the prospect of lung cancer does not apply to them. They are easily led by 'conspiracy' advertising – the kind in which, for example, they recognize an un-named brand and feel good for having done so – and will reinforce that brand message amongst their friends. Hook a few young smokers and it snowballs. They are also great watchers of the sponsored sports on television, so there is no difficulty getting the brand name through to them. To a far greater extent than adults, children smoke the most heavily advertised brands and this is even reflected in regional differences in response to regional advertising. A third to a half of 11–15-year-olds who try cigarettes become regular smokers.

Most children, with their self-confidence, trust in the world and boundless optimism, are no match for clever publicity; older and more cynical people might realize the advert is aimed at them, look behind the message and ask 'what's in it for the advertiser?' There seems little commercial justification for spending much of the advertising budget on adults.

So who do the real tobacco companies target? Regular smoking (at least one cigarette per week) amongst 15-year-olds in the UK is currently running at nearly the average adult figure of 28%. Norway provides a telling example; in 1975, when 17% of its 13–15-year-olds were smoking at least one cigarette per day, tobacco advertising was banned. By 1990, the figure had dropped to 10%. Subsequently it has risen and the Norwegian government is now tightening up on hidden advertising such as sports sponsorship.

US: legal moves

The recent legal successes against tobacco companies in the US have opened the floodgates to hitherto confidential information. All along, whilst swearing on oath before a Congressional Committee on the health hazards of tobacco that 'nicotine is not addictive', tobacco company executives have apparently been discussing the commercial value of the addictiveness of nicotine and aiming their adverts at children. They are now earmarking vast sums in the future to pay claims (out of court) for damage to health caused by smoking, in return for not being sued.

'OK, guv, it's a fair cop, but I'll only pay up if everyone pretends it wasn't my fault.'

As long as they pay up, does this matter? The answer depends on what you want to see happen. If they could be sued they might be ruined and the whole edifice would crumble. Setting aside profits to pay compensation means they have to go on making a profit, which they do by recruiting enough new smokers to replace the dead ones. The cost of compensating those who are ill now through smoking is being borne by those who are going to be ill through smoking.

The prospect of tobacco companies going bankrupt as a result of being sued in the US is possibly naïve, not because of any inability of the US courts to impose staggering financial penalties but because the companies have seen this coming and are, to a certain extent, backing away from developed countries as their financial power base. In the emerging nations there are far more people who are less cynical about advertising and less aware of health issues, and there are far fewer restrictions on commercial activity.

Developing markets

Whilst smoking in many developed countries is creeping downwards as people become more aware of the risks they are running, and tobacco advertising is being squeezed down or banned outright, it is increasing hugely in Africa, the Middle East and much of the Far East.

China is by far the greatest producer of tobacco in the world. In 1990, China grew 36% of the approximately 7 million tonne world tobacco crop, the US 9.7%, Brazil 6.7%, India 6.1% and Turkey 3%. With about 21% of the world's 5.4 billion population (1991), China's 36% of world tobacco production looks disproportionate, but the US has less than 5% of the world's population compared with its 9.7% of world tobacco production.

A lot of tobacco is consumed in China; 464 million (40%) of the 1.1 billion population are smokers, with far more men than women smoking. However, there are signs that things could be changing. In some parts of China an extra sales tax soon to be imposed on tobacco products will be used to fund health promotion and anti-smoking campaigns. In the medical literature, plenty of papers are now being published by Chinese authors on smoking and health, and Western businessmen returning from trips to China report the odd factory where smoking is not permitted. In one at least, it was not even permitted out of doors on factory premises, so the employees' only chance for a drag all day was to go off site during the lunch break.

In 1915, when British American Tobacco first got into China, tobacco consumption was extremely low. By 1945 it was firmly established, with an average consumption of roughly 200 cigarettes per year for every man, woman and child in the country: a triumph of marketing, or the natural spread of a pleasurable but addictive habit? By 1966, Chinese cigarette production was nearer 1,500 per head of population per annum.

After the second world war, in 1945, America began a 'food for peace' program which included exporting tobacco, thus exposing the people of numerous developing countries to the tobacco habits of the West. However, before indignation at this deliberate foisting of a deadly, addictive and lucrative product onto millions boils over, it is as well to remember that the link between smoking and lung cancer – the first disease proven to be smoking-related – was only formally made in 1950 when large surveys of the lifestyle and habits of lung cancer victims were published, one each in Britain and the US, and only confirmed by subsequent careful and lengthy work. Two generations later, we are still uncovering adverse health consequences of smoking.

Moral Aspects

The moral position of the tobacco trade gets a bit murkier as time goes on and ignorance is no longer an excuse. In the 1980s the US government threatened trade sanctions against some Asian countries unless they opened up to American cigarettes. Thailand has managed to ban advertising but in the year after American cigarettes arrived in Taiwan, cigarette consumption rose by 5%.

In most developing nations there are at present few controls on tobacco advertising, no health warnings on packets of cigarettes, little health education targeted on smoking and enormous pressure to encourage tobacco production and consumption.

Power of the multi-nationals

Four big multi-national tobacco conglomerates dominate world tobacco trade, with 30% of it between them. They are Philip Morris and RJ Reynolds (US), BAT Industries (UK) and Japan Tobacco. They are wealthier than many of the smaller nations in which they operate and can increase the governments' desperately needed foreign currency earnings from exports as well as create jobs at home. They are able to offer a complete package for starting up tobacco production, from expertise to loans to meet the initial costs of seed, fertilizer, pesticides and capital equipment such as, for example, curing barns. By locking the farmers into debt, they keep a tight hold over them.

On a family level, the consequences of smoking can be severe. As an example, in Bangladesh 60% of men (and 15% of women, though this is rising) smoke. For many families, budgets are so tight that the cost of one person smoking just a few cigarettes a day can reduce the amount of food available to the children.

Smoking is the direct cause of a large proportion of fires (the King's Cross underground fire was probably started by a discarded match) and in countries where people live in dwellings made of wood and other burnable materials, smoking poses a particular threat.

Subsidies for tobacco growers

The World Bank and the UN Food and Agriculture Organization, amongst others, have in the past supported tobacco as a cash crop in poor countries. However, in 1992 the World Bank stopped granting loans for tobacco. Though there are undoubted short-term gains to be had, the long-term costs were felt to outweigh these.

The EU still subsidizes tobacco, mainly in Italy and Greece. The Common Agricultural Policy spends about £900 million a year propping up tobacco production, the quality of which is mainly too poor for European tastes. It is very high in tar and is sold off to developing countries.

Environmental effects

Tobacco cultivation has environmental impact beyond the problems associated with clearing an area of native plants and covering it with a single non-native crop. As an example, in Malawi, most of the fuel used is wood and deforestation for fuel is a serious problem. Twenty-three percent of the wood used goes on curing tobacco, which is a major export crop. There is also concern about the environmental impact of pesticides and fertilizers used to raise tobacco.

Health and mortality

Ultimately, the health of these nations will suffer. Already in Pakistan, deaths from lung cancer have overtaken all other cancers. In India, a huge increase in smoking has been accompanied by a six-fold rise in people dying from chronic obstructive pulmonary disease (bronchitis and emphysema). Because control of the tobacco industries is much less stringent in some of the developing countries than in, for example, Europe, cigarettes tend to be stronger, with higher tar levels, so the disease they engender will be swifter and more extensive.

The World Bank expects smoking to increase by 12% in poorer countries between 1990 and 2000, while it drops in industrialized countries as a result of better education and tighter controls on advertising.

Medical statistics show a starker picture. In 1995, 3 million deaths worldwide were caused by smoking, 2 million in developed countries and 1 million in developing countries. In 2025 or thereabouts, there will be 10 million deaths from smoking, with a 50% increase to 3 million in developed countries and a staggering 7-fold increase to 7 million in developing countries. The calculation is not based on some projection of smoking habits. It is the death toll in people who are smokers at the time of writing.

CHAPTER 3
Tobacco smoke

Nicotine makes a useful pesticide

Around 700 chemical compounds exist in the leaves of the tobacco plant but when it has been cured, processed, blended, packaged and lit up, some 4000 emerge in the smoke. A few of them are totally harmless (for example water vapour), others are irritants or antigens (substances which provoke the immune system into making antibodies as part of a strategy for getting rid of them), some are downright toxic (for example hydrogen cyanide, some heavy metals such as cadmium and lead) and a small proportion are highly dangerous, including mutagens (chemical or radioactive compounds, for example polonium 210, capable of causing genetic damage which is perpetuated as cells divide), carcinogens (cancer-causing substances), at least one of which, benzo[a]pyrene, is extremely potent, and co-carcinogens (substances which enhance the power of carcinogens to cause cancer).

Some components of smoke do their damage directly, in which case the amount of harm caused will roughly depend on the quantity that gets into the body, whilst the effects of others can escalate. A simple irritant might fit into the first group while a carcinogen, which modifies a minute amount of tissue so that it grows out of control and eventually becomes cancer, belongs in the second. An antigen could well be a bit of both, so rather than two distinct groups, these are two ends of a continuous range of harmful effects.

The other difference between the two ends of the range is that at the direct end, the effect follows swiftly on the arrival of the agent, whereas at the other end, damage done today can lie hidden, emerging into disease (for example a noticeable tumor) in many years' time.

Tobacco smoke is a mixture of gases, vapours (which tend to condense) and particles which, at less than two thousandths of a millimetre across (1/25th of the diameter of a human hair), are so small that they can get right into the tiniest parts of the lungs. The particles and most of the condensable components of the smoke are together known as tar. Nicotine, although arguably a component of tar, is so important to smokers that it is generally considered separately.

Gases in smoke

The gases make up over half of the volume of smoke and include several which are known to be damaging to body tissues. The more familiar ones are as follows.

Formaldehyde

Formalin, a 37% solution of formaldehyde in water, is to be found pickling many biological specimens worldwide and even the odd exhibit in the Tate Gallery. In lesser concentrations than those used for preserving tissue (preservation involves killing all living tissues present) it is very irritant. Acrolein, another but less familiar aldehyde in tobacco smoke, is even more irritant to lung tissues than is formaldehyde.

Acetaldehyde

One of the more toxic intermediate products of the fermentation by yeast to produce alcohol (ethanol) in beer, wine etc., and also a breakdown product of alcohol in the body, it is responsible for some of the more damaging effects of heavy drinking.

Methanol

The drinking of methanol (meths, also known as wood alcohol), results in blindness due to destruction of the optic nerve. Even prolonged skin exposure or inhalation can have the same effect.

Acetone

This is nail varnish remover and also a useful industrial solvent. It will strip the varnish from modern 'non-tarnishing' brass door handles etc., allowing them to be polished.

Ammonia

Used in fertilizers, explosives, cleaning fluids, synthetic fibres and smash-and-grab raids, long-term exposure to even low levels of inhaled ammonia can produce irritation of lung tissues.

Nitrogen dioxide

Used in making nitric acid and rocket fuel, it is highly poisonous as a gas because it irritates the lung tissues and can cause oedema (swelling) in the lungs, which decreases the amount of air the lungs can take in and makes it harder for the oxygen to get through to the blood. An unwelcome by-product when coal is burned at high temperatures, to reduce its emission from coal fired power stations the combustion temperature has to be kept below 850°C. It is also given off when grass is fermented into silage.

Hydrogen sulphide

This toxic gas is best known from rotten eggs and stink bombs.

Hydrogen cyanide

Also known as prussic acid, it is one of the fastest-acting poisons because it gets inside cells and prevents them using oxygen. It is thus lethal to many forms of life and is used for fumigating buildings and sterilizing soil. The 'bitter almonds' smell makes frequent appearances in crime novels, but its darkest part in human history is its use as an agent of mass murder in gas chambers.

These are all very disturbing things to find in tobacco smoke but as people clearly don't drop down dead at the first drag, they can't be in grossly dangerous concentrations. The hydrogen cyanide is a good example: cyanide becomes toxic (i.e. noticeably poisonous) to humans when its level in whole blood reaches 1000 micrograms (millionths of a gram) per litre (μg/l). Ordinary healthy non-smokers average 16 $\mu g/l$ and smokers 41 $\mu g/l$. This is far from instant death, though it is nibbling at the margins of good health. If it were the only damaging component in tobacco smoke, its effect would probably be hardly noticeable, but it is just one of many substances in tobacco smoke whose effect is to deprive cells of the use of oxygen.

Carbon monoxide

The one gas which stands out from the rest as individually dangerous in the quantities inhaled when smoking is carbon monoxide. As a chemical compound it is midway between the oxygen molecule O_2 (which we need for energy) and the carbon dioxide molecule CO_2 (waste from energy production), being a carbon atom with only one oxygen atom attached, CO. As such, it is able to hop on board the transport system for oxygen and carbon dioxide in the blood and, once there, it is very difficult to get rid of, with the result that oxygen is in short supply. Those smoking more than 40 cigarettes a day can have a CO level which is 10–20 times that of non-smokers, half of the toxic level and 20% of the lethal level. (Lethal levels are generally defined as the level of exposure which would kill half the people exposed.)

Carbon monoxide is produced by the burning of the tobacco, but some cigarette filters actually increase the carbon monoxide yield of cigarettes.

Away from tobacco smoke, carbon monoxide is found in coal gas (but not in natural gas) and in exhaust fumes, and is given off during the burning of many fuels, especially if there is limited oxygen available. It is responsible for a number of deaths annually of people burning gas heaters with blocked flues, so the exhaust fumes come out into the room. If the room is poorly ventilated, the person and the fire are competing for the available oxygen. Carbon monoxide has no colour and no smell, and the feeling of lethargy and sleepiness is by no means out of the ordinary when sitting by the fire.

Nicotine

The most important constituent by far, from the point of view of smokers as well as those whose livelihood is tobacco, is nicotine.

Pure nicotine is a colourless, odourless, oily liquid but when exposed to air it soon turns brown and smells of tobacco. It is soluble in water as well as alcohol and oil, which means it can get swiftly to most parts of the body. It can get in through the gut (if swallowed) and skin (on direct contact) as well as via the mouth and lungs.

Commercial tobacco crops contain 2–8% nicotine. Out in the tobacco fields, when the dew is on the leaves, nicotine leaches out into the drops of moisture and onto the hands and arms of the pickers. As it is absorbed readily through the skin, workers not wearing protective gloves suffer 'green tobacco sickness': dizziness, nausea, vomiting and prostration.

Chemically, nicotine is very close to niacin, one of the B-group vitamins familiar from the side of the cornflake box. Niacin is also known as nicotinic acid and as vitamin PP, and can be made from nicotine by adding nitric acid, although commercially it is made from extracts of coal tar.

Niacin is the anti-pellagra vitamin, pellagra being a condition in which the gut and skin are disturbed and there are nervous and mental disorders. As niacin is so vital to the proper working of these areas, it is hardly surprising that its close chemical cousin nicotine can also get in (many molecules gain access to structures by physically fitting an entry site, a bit like a key in a lock), though it cannot do niacin's job.

Greenhouse pesticide

Nicotine is sufficiently poisonous to kill, and this makes it a very useful pesticide; reasonably achievable quantities will kill virtually anything that moves. Its main use is in enclosed spaces such as greenhouses and mushroom houses. It is available for spraying but also as fumigant 'shreds', which are bits of cardboard impregnated with nicotine. Poisonous fumigants are in some ways safer to handle than poisonous sprays, because the operator can get out of the way before most of the action takes place.

The technique is to don full protective clothing – overalls, rubber gloves and respirator – and lay small heaps along the path in the greenhouse. Starting from the far end and working back towards the door, each pile is set alight with a blowtorch. The flames are then extinguished and the piles left to smoulder, when the nicotine is vapourized into the air.

The greenhouse then has to be left closed for 12 hours, during which time no-one without protective gear should enter. It is generally done overnight and the next morning all surfaces are littered with dead greenfly, leaf miners, sawflies, woolly aphids and all their friends and relations – unless, of course, the greenhouse is properly managed, in which case there is a modest sprinkling of corpses.

Nicotine in the fields

Before the days of organophosphates (cheap, widely used and famous for their role in the Gulf War), nicotine, extracted from tobacco scraps, was sprayed on crops in fields. At least one farmer decided that he could make his own more cheaply than buying it, so he planted a small crop of tobacco, shredded it, steeped the shreddings in water and sprayed the resultant liquor on the crops. It worked a treat but, unfortunately for him, HM Customs and Excise got wind of it and paid the farm a visit.

After some discussion as to whether what they were growing was 'just rubbish' (farmer), or a viable smoking tobacco crop subject to Customs and Excise duty, the Inspector agreed to an expert opinion and duly sent off a sample to a UK cigarette manufacturer. Much to the farmer's dismay, it turned out to be high quality cigarette tobacco and the cheapest option was to go back to buying nicotine insecticide commercially.

Because nicotine is broken down in light and water, it is held to be a relatively safe pesticide for humans to use on crops. Regulations demand that no harvesting should take place for a set time after treatment (24 or 48 hours, depending on the crop) but after that time any residue is supposed to be harmless.

However, though safe for crops, nicotine is deadly to insects, pretty damaging to birds and animals and extremely toxic in rivers. Fish are very easily killed by it and so are the water-dwelling creatures they live on; a small spill of nicotine into a stream can kill miles of river.

Pollution of rivers is now very tightly monitored and analytical methods have become extremely sensitive; so sensitive that nicotine from the fingers of a smoker involved in the sampling of a river pollution incident under investigation can show up as a definite blip in the analysis.

Gourmet's delight?

The ability of nicotine to kill aquatic life is used in Spain, where elvers (baby eels), thin wriggly worm-like creatures not much longer than a finger, are a highly expensive delicacy. Born in the Sargasso sea off the Gulf of Mexico, they make their way across the Atlantic, drifting with the Gulf Stream, and enter the rivers of the west coast of Europe in huge numbers. They convert from salt water to fresh water and spend years growing to adulthood in the rivers, where many of them provide food for other water creatures. The survivors return as adult eels to the Atlantic and the cycle continues. Amongst their predators are humans, lurking on the river banks in the dead of night with hand-held nets or trawling the estuaries with fine mesh.

Unlike most fish, as long as their gills are wet, elvers (and eels) can breathe air. Indeed, they can live easily out of water for 24 hours if kept damp and cool, which means they can be transported live to the markets of cities and served fresh to the customers. Nicotine is the chosen agent for killing them. A chunk of rough black 'mountain tobacco' shag is stirred up in some water and the liquid strained off. The elvers are put into tanks of water and the tobacco liquid added. They react by producing large quantities of 'vomp', a frothy slime which leaves hands chapped and cracked, which can then be rinsed away leaving freshly killed elvers in perfect condition for frying in oil and garlic.

Toxicity and addiction

Because of its use as a pesticide, nicotine's toxicity has been studied in depth on a number of animals as well as man. It causes developmental defects in rat embryos, especially causing damage to the brain and nervous system.

It also reduces fertility in adult rats to such an extent that the population given nicotine died out after one generation. The mechanisms involved inflammatory processes and increases in the numbers of inflammatory cells, i.e. the same mechanism that causes such damage to the lungs, blood vessels and, in all probability, other tissues in human smokers.

In mice, quantities equivalent to a human smoking 10-30 cigarettes per day can significantly impair sperm production.

In humans, nicotine (in pregnant women smokers) can cross the placenta and gain access to the developing baby. It is also found in the breast milk of smoking mothers.

In cigarette-smoking quantities, nicotine has a stimulant effect on the brain. It has long been believed to have a sedative effect at higher concentrations, but this is an erroneous view due to misinterpretation of early observations on rats, whose reduction in activity in response to higher doses of nicotine were almost certainly due to its toxicity. Though the rats looked laid back and tranquil, they were almost certainly suffering a degree of paralysis.

Subjectively, smoking can be either invigorating or stress-relieving and relaxing, but its effect will depend on many factors including the smoker's state of mind at the time. It's rather like expecting to enhance the flavour of lunch by spreading pickle on it – it might work wonders on the bread and cheese but is unlikely to do the same for a banana split.

There have been occasional outbursts of fierce debate among scientists as to whether nicotine is addictive in the strict pharmacological sense. Aside from the problem that addiction is a term difficult to define, part of the basis for the debate is that nicotine, unlike, for example, cocaine, is not very pleasurable to someone not dependent on it. However, the US Surgeon-General's 1988 report on nicotine addiction concluded that cigarettes and tobacco are addictive, that nicotine is the drug which causes addiction and that its addictive qualities are similar to those of drugs like heroin and cocaine. In particular, the symptoms of withdrawl from nicotine are comparable to those of other major drugs of abuse. Parts of the tobacco industry have now also admitted in public that smoking is addictive, even though previously they had vehemently denied it, so the academic debate no longer has any value to the tobacco lobby.

Nicotine in slightly higher concentrations is a rapidly acting poison in humans. The nicotine content varies between cigarettes but 50 mg, i.e. the nicotine from half a dozen average cigarettes, placed on the tongue, would kill the average adult. (The nicotine yield, that which the smoker absorbs, is around 1 mg per cigarette.) The symptoms begin with feeling sick and dizzy and with emptying of the bladder and bowel, and proceed rapidly to fits and choking. In fatal cases, death is usually within an hour and occurs because the respiratory system is paralysed.

Medical uses

Until recently, there was little medical use for nicotine. However, nicotine replacement, delivered via cigarette-like tubes to suck through, chewing gum or patches on the skin, is available to help smokers give up. In addition, some anecdotal reports of benefits from smoking in some medical conditions have led to studies with nicotine.

Tar

One of the Ironbridge Gorge Museums, near Telford, Shropshire, is a tar tunnel. This is natural tar associated with the coal seams above, and it had many uses in the industrial era of 18th century Britain. For a modest charge, visitors can don a hard hat and stoop along the horizontal shaft which was the entrance to a tar mine and see the tar still oozing, wet and black, through the roof and walls. It is almost like being inside the windpipe of a giant heavy smoker – dead, of course, as it's cold and still – except for the rails where the tar trucks used to run.

Coal tar

Nowadays, coal tar is produced when coal is heated (to 900–1200°C, in the absence of air) to make coke. The vapours which are driven off by the heat are condensed to form tar, the diverse industrial uses of which include the manufacture of synthetic drugs (including nicotine's close cousin, the B-group vitamin niacin), perfumes, dyes, soap, disinfectants and waterproofing compounds for building.

Wood tar

Wood tar is a similar by-product when wood is heated to make charcoal, and different woods give different kinds of tar. The pine forests of Sweden, Finland and Russia have traditionally produced large quantities of distillates from resinous woods, from which turpentine oil (which was mainly used in paint and varnish, though less toxic substitutes are now preferred) emerges as a clear thin liquid leaving the much heavier and darker tar. This was the stuff of Jolly Jack Tar, which he mixed with hemp fibre to make oakum for jamming into the gaps between the ship's timbers, or soaked into twine and rope to increase their life and strength at sea. He even held his pigtail together with it, so that the wisps of hair didn't blow into his mouth while he was chewing his baccy.

Gas-oil tar

Gas-oil tar is the last gooey fragment when crude oil is fractionally distilled to separate such components as petrol/gasoline, kerosene, diesel, heavier oils and finally tar. The very densest and toughest part of the tar is asphalt, nowadays used as the main waterproofing agent in such things as roofing felt, and as the sticky part of the crushed

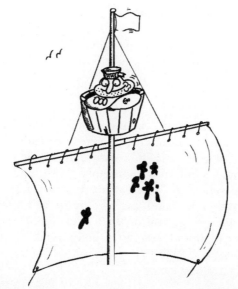

Jolly Jack Tar . . . while he was chewing his baccy

stone mixture in road surfaces.

All these tars have one thing in common: they came originally from plant or animal life. Coal is what is left of plant matter which has slowly decomposed in swampy conditions (no oxygen) and been squashed under successive layers of sediment and rock over about 300 million years, and petroleum is the incompletely decomposed liquid remains of plant and animal matter, lying pooled between layers of rock, generally with water beneath and natural gas above it. Little wonder, then, that when dried plant matter is heated and the vapours drawn off as by dragging on a cigarette, they condense into tar on every available surface. Most plants will produce tarry vapours when burned (smokers of 'herbal' tobaccos take note); what singles out tobacco is the nicotine.

Toxic contents of tobacco tar

The particles of tar which line the living rooms and lungs of smokers contain many hazardous substances. The polycyclic hydrocarbons include many well-documented carcinogens including benzo[a]-pyrene, a potent human carcinogen. More carcinogens are among the nitrosamines and aromatic amines also present. In all, about 60 known or suspected carcinogens are present in cigarette smoke.

The heavy metals also deserve mention. Two in particular are a cause for concern to smokers: cadmium and lead. They, with mercury, are the most toxic to humans of the heavy metal environmental pollutants.

Cadmium

Tobacco plants concentrate cadmium from the soil in their leaves, and tobacco smoke is an important source of cadmium in humans. Since much of it goes into sidestream smoke, it is of concern to passive smokers. Cadmium is highly toxic, with injury to kidney and lung tissue as well as to other areas. It gains access to the fetus developing in the womb and is excreted in the breast milk of smoking mothers. It is hard to get rid of; even if cadmium intake stops, the time taken for cadmium levels in the body to fall by 50% is between 10 and 30 years.

Lead

Smokers have higher lead levels in their blood than do non-smokers. Most of the lead in the body passes eventually to bone, where it accumulates. Lead is toxic to all people, attacking the digestive system, muscle and kidney. However, its effect on children is of particular concern because it can cause serious developmental problems in the brain, leading to mental retardation, seizures and even death. Most of the lead in cigarette smoke is in sidestream smoke, making passive smoking important. Children living with smokers have higher blood lead levels than do children living smoke-free; having smoking parents poses a higher risk than living near a lead smelting plant.

Mercury

Whilst mercury, another important heavy metal environmental pollutant, is present in cigarette smoke, smoking does not appear to increase levels in the body.

Differences between individuals

When cigarettes are tested in government laboratories to measure the constituents in their smoke, standardized smoking machines are used and give repeatable results.

People smoke differently; dragging hard increases the burning temperature, short puffs give a different smoke composition from longer ones and the first couple of drags through a filter-tipped cigarette have very much less tar and nicotine in them than do the last few.

The detailed composition of smoke varies not only with how the cigarette is smoked, but also with the type of tobacco and additives used, so that it is difficult to predict the effects of smoking from considering the individual substances present. The best we can do, in practical terms, is look at typical damage and relate it back to what we know is in smoke. This approach allows us to focus on the small proportion of the 4000-odd substances which we think do the most damage.

However, people vary, too, in their ability to cope with what enters their bodies. Some suffer hay fever when they breathe pollen, others don't; some have an attack of migraine when they eat certain foods, others are unaffected; and doubtless some are more susceptible than others to substances in tobacco smoke. This helps explain why smoking only kills half of smokers and why some die of cancer whilst others die of circulatory disease, why some lose a leg to gangrene whilst others are just rather unfit.

Chapter 4

Where does the smoke go?

Into the lungs, then blood

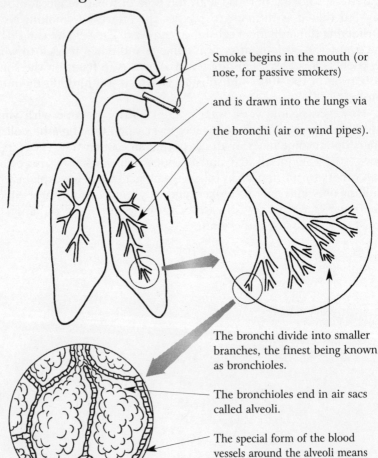

Smoke begins in the mouth (or nose, for passive smokers)

and is drawn into the lungs via

the bronchi (air or wind pipes).

The bronchi divide into smaller branches, the finest being known as bronchioles.

The bronchioles end in air sacs called alveoli.

The special form of the blood vessels around the alveoli means that the blood flows in thin sheets over the whole alveolar surface.

This arrangement spreads the incoming air over a huge surface of very thin tissue, the other side of which is blood, and it is here that gases are exchanged between air and blood. In a pair of healthy adult lungs, the gas exchange surface has roughly the same area as a tennis court. Spread over such an area, all the air in the lungs is close to the blood, so the molecules of gas can move quickly from one to the other. Many of the chemicals in smoke pass straight through from the alveoli into the blood.

The blood takes on oxygen (essential for the chemical reactions producing energy in our cells) and off-loads carbon dioxide (a waste product of the energy-producing reactions). To keep the lungs working efficiently, the air is warmed and humidified as it comes in down the airways, so it is important for the airways to stay in good condition. What we breathe out is warmer, moister, lower in oxygen and higher in carbon dioxide than what we breathe in.

The features which allow for rapid oxygen and carbon dioxide exchange in the lungs also make it quick and easy for smoke chemicals to get into the blood.

All around the body

The left side of the heart takes blood enriched with oxygen, and loaded with smoke chemicals, from the lungs and pumps it round the rest of the body. The right side of the heart collects blood from the rest of the body and pumps it to the lungs.

The whole body is thus exposed to the chemicals from smoke. They spread quickly; from lungs to brain takes about 8 seconds.

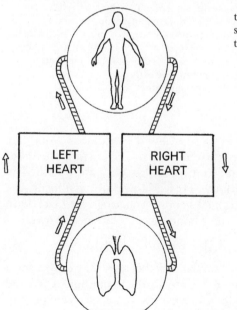

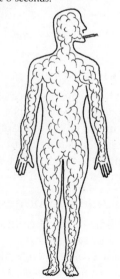

Some gets out again

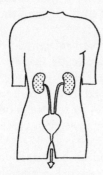
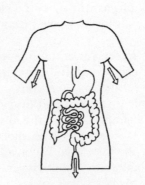
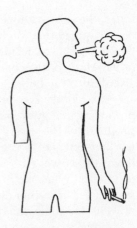

The main exit route for the smoke chemicals, many of which are broken down in the body, is via the kidneys and bladder in urine.

Small quantities leave via the skin in sweat, or via the gut with the rest of our food waste.

Some is breathed back out.

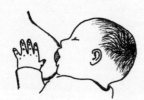

Mothers who smoke and are breast feeding also excrete some smoke chemicals in their milk. Nicotine is more concentrated in their breast milk than in their blood, and the breast milk of a heavy smoker can contain 0.5 mg of nicotine (half a smoked cigarette's worth) per litre, as well as cadmium, lead and other toxic chemicals.

Some stays

The body takes time to get rid of unwanted substances. Some are gone within hours but others stay for years. Those components of smoke which cannot be cleared out as fast as they are breathed in simply build up inside the body. This is especially visible in the mouth, where the teeth are stained yellow. The lungs are black with tar in long-term smokers and their bones accumulate heavy metals.

Some components of smoke cause trouble

Some of the chemicals from the smoke, whether they stay only a short while or build up and take years to go, are hostile to our bodies. We did not evolve to cope with breathing tobacco smoke and so have poor or no protection against some of its harmful effects. The result is disease.

CHAPTER 5
Lungs, airways and bloodstream

Material in this chapter is presented in more detail in Appendix I

Smoker's cough

Every time anyone breathes cigarette smoke, body tissues are damaged. This is not what the cigarette ads say and certainly not what most smokers believe, but nevertheless it is a fact.

Part of the harm is caused by smoke acting directly on living tissues but, even more seriously, tobacco smoke provokes some of the body's defence agents into attacking the structures they normally protect and repair: elastic lung tissue gets eaten away, and the highly specialized linings of blood vessels, which are essential for maintaining healthy blood flow, are damaged.

Repairs can take place if the levels of smoke chemicals die down, but the next cigarette raises them again. Some of the damage, in both lungs and blood vessels, cannot be reversed. It builds up, unnoticed, over the years.

Lungs and airways

Because they take the smoke directly, the lungs are badly affected in cigarette smokers, particularly because the direct damage done by the smoke is multiplied by the lungs' own defences; driven out of control by the smoke, they destroy lung tissue.

Lung tissue eaten away (emphysema)

Inflammatory phagocytes (scavenger cells)

Deep inside the lungs are teams of freely-moving scavenger cells whose job is to keep the lung tissues clean. They do this by eating any unwanted matter – dust, germs and suchlike – and then squeezing through into the bloodstream and carrying it away. They are part of the white cell population in blood, and similar scavenger cells can be found in most parts of the body. Their ability to eat things gives them their name, phagocytes (Greek, literally 'eater cells'). They are described as inflammatory because it is they that bring about inflammation, part of the healing response to injury or infection. Inside them are powerful chemicals (enzymes) for killing and digesting germs.

Phagocytes behaving badly . . .

When smoke arrives they become excited (scientists describe them as 'angry'), and some of the chemicals get spilled. These start to break down the lung tissue . . .

. . . but worse is to come. Healthy lung tissue is protected from normal occasional spillage by another chemical, found in the fluid lining the lung tissues, which neutralizes any enzymes spilled. This chemical doesn't work properly in smokers, so their lungs are wide open to attack.

Direct damage to the lungs, caused by oxidants and other chemicals in the smoke, add to the problem. Outside the body, oxidation is also known as corrosion and rusting.

. . . and inviting their mates round

Perhaps worst of all from the smoker's point of view, when the phagocytes get angry they signal for help, so in come more of the same cells plus some far more vicious specialist germ-killer cells. These have about 100 times as much of the tissue-digesting enzyme, and they, too, spill it in response to smoke.

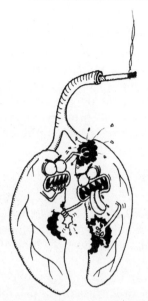

Eating away at themselves

Smokers' lungs contain nearly twice as many of the milder phagocytes as do non-smokers' lungs, but in addition they have the very powerful ones which are not normally found in healthy lungs. With every inhalation of smoke, a few more burst and spill their devastating enzymes, only to be replaced by fresh ones from the blood.

Coughs and colds?

For anyone, smoker or non-smoker, having a cough or cold increases the number of phagocytes in the lungs, at which time smoking, including passive smoking, is even more to be avoided than usual.

When the elastic goes

Much of what is being destroyed is the elastic tissue in the lungs. Healthy alveoli are like tiny balloons, and most of the muscular effort in breathing is made as we breathe in; breathing out is helped by the natural elasticity of the alveoli squeezing out the air. (The fact that the lungs are fixed inside the ribcage stops them emptying completely; if they did so, to get them inflated again would require great effort – just like getting a balloon started.) When alveoli have had their elasticity destroyed, they behave more like plastic bags than balloons: they can be filled with air but they don't empty themselves.

41

Emphysema creeps up unnoticed . . .

The name given to this disease of the lungs is emphysema. It starts happening as soon as a person starts smoking, but it creeps up unnoticed. Because lungs can cope with far more than our normal level of activity (most of us can, if we have to, run uphill), we normally only use a small proportion of our lung capacity. Most smokers don't notice they have emphysema until about half their lung tissue has been destroyed.

. . . and has no cure

It is irreversible – the elastic tissue never grows back – and there is no way of repairing the damage. Emphysematous patches, because they tend to be kept over-inflated by healthy alveoli emptying into them, can squeeze neighbouring healthy bits of lung, preventing them working properly.

The symptoms can be eased with bronchodilator drugs to relax the airways and make breathing as easy as possible (similar to treatment of asthma attacks), and with physiotherapy. Antibiotics are needed regularly to cope with the frequent infections in the damaged tissues.

It is possible, if the emphysema is confined to some parts of the lung and not others, to surgically remove the worst bits and thus relieve the pressure on the less damaged areas. This is a major operation, involving cutting through ribs to open up the chest wall. It is not suitable for all sufferers, and carries risks as well as potential benefits, but it can improve matters for some.

Sufferers from advanced emphysema live their lives in wheel-chairs, an oxygen cylinder and mask close to hand, dependent on nebulizers so they can inhale aerosols of drugs. John Huston, who died of emphysema, carried a small oxygen pack on his back to enable him to direct his last film. Most smokers in poor countries, the current growth area in cigarette sales, do not have access to such help.

Quitting

Giving up smoking, while it cannot reverse the damage done, will stop the emphysema progressing further.

Airways damaged (bronchitis)

Smoker's cough

Chemicals in the smoke directly attack the airway lining, making it raw, red and irritable, the condition known as bronchitis. In regular smokers, the oxidants, irritants and poisons never stop coming, and the condition becomes permanent. This is known as chronic bronchitis.

Lining the airways is a layer of mucus, which acts as a sticky trap for dust, germs and suchlike. It also contains antibodies to fight germs. The mucus is kept moving by a layer of tiny 'fingers' covering the surface of the airways. Their tips move in waves, carrying the mucus up until it reaches the throat, where it can be swallowed or coughed out.

Tobacco smoke paralyses these fingers. With the aid of a microscope, they can be seen wilting as the smoke passes over them, though they recover in clean air. Continued smoking makes the paralysis permanent, so the mucus has to be coughed up. Smoking also poisons the cells which make the mucus, so they make thicker mucus and more of it, with fewer antibodies.

'Smoker's cough' is the familiar result. It worsens emphysema by tearing the weakened lung tissues.

Coughs and colds: germs on hang-gliders

Not only are smokers more prone to pick up the germs which cause coughs and colds, they are also very efficient at spreading them. When they cough or sneeze them out, the germs come riding on smoke particles. It's like putting them on hang-gliders – they can soar in the air for a hundred times as long as germs sneezed out by non-smokers, making them far more likely to infect someone else.

The ability of smokers to aid the spread of respiratory infections to others is one of the less obvious risks of passive smoking. Infants are particularly vulnerable.

Lung cancer . . .

The best known of the health risks of smoking, lung cancer was the first to be established, with two important studies being published in the US and the UK in 1950. Lung cancer was an extremely rare disease before smoking was common. When the news about smoking and lung cancer broke, smoking among doctors and scientists dropped but there was little impact on the general population.

Lung cancer now causes more deaths than any other kind of cancer, in women as well as in men. Nine out of ten lung cancer deaths are caused by smoking, and some of the remaining deaths are due to passive smoking.

. . . creeps up unnoticed

Smoke contains many carcinogens, and they get deep into the lungs. Lung cancer, like emphysema, develops unnoticed. Most lung cancer isn't diagnosed until the chance of a cure is only one in fifty.

Lung cancer, vitamin E and selenium

A recent Japanese study has shown that lung cancer patients have reduced levels of vitamin E and the element selenium in their lungs. Furthermore, members of their families also have lower levels than non-smokers.

Whether the levels of vitamin E and selenium are reduced by smoking and passive smoking, or reflect family eating habits, and whether lung cancer is more likely to develop in these conditions, or whether the finding is just a coincidence, are important questions posed but not answered by this study. Further research could yield useful information about how lung cancer develops in smokers.

Women at greater risk than men

Women took up smoking about 20 years later than men, and the rise in lung cancer among women has been correspondingly delayed. Although the number of women smokers in developed countries has begun to fall, lung cancer among women is still rising. The increasing number of female deaths from lung cancer has recently allowed detailed comparisons between men and women. It seems that women may be more likely (three times more so in one study) than men with the same smoking history to die of lung cancer.

Starting young increases the risk

It is clear from some studies carried out in the US that the younger a person starts smoking the greater are the risks of lung cancer.

Males starting to smoke at 15 years of age are twice as likely to die of lung cancer as those who begin between 20 and 24 and four to five times as likely as those who begin after the age of 25.

Quite why the young smoker is more vulnerable than the older one is not yet clear. A reasonable possibility is that during development, cells are particularly vulnerable to genetic damage; in adulthood, when physical development is complete, carcinogens may have less to work on.

The situation with females is unlikely to be any better, especially as women who smoke seem to run a greater risk of getting lung cancer than men. Only time will tell, because the women who began smoking in increasing numbers over the last 30 years will be providing the lung cancer statistics during the next 30 years.

Risk for all smokers

- smoking for 20 years is 16 times as likely to result in lung cancer as giving up after 10
- those who smoke 25 cigarettes or more per day are three times more likely to die of lung cancer than those who smoke fewer than 15 per day
- heavy smokers run a 35 times greater risk than non-smokers
- 90% of lung cancer is caused by smoking, and some of the remainder by passive smoking

The risk falls after quitting

Not all the news is bad. After quitting, the risk of lung cancer (indeed, of nearly all smoking-related diseases) falls, though the rate at which it falls varies with how long and how much someone has smoked. After 20 cigarettes a day for 20 years, three years' abstinence is needed before the lung cancer risk begins to drop and 10–15 years before it is back to that of a non-smoker.

These figures are over all smokers, irrespective of the age at which they started. There is as yet no evidence on whether those who started young can recoup their position in the same time as those who started later in life, but it doesn't look like a safe bet.

Mouth and throat

Cancer of the mouth and throat are very much related to tobacco use of all types. Only about a quarter of deaths from cancer of the mouth and throat are not smoking-related, though this ignores the effects of tobacco chewing and snuff dipping, which are rare habits, though of recent increase, in developed countries where the bulk of the research is done. In Britain, about 2500 cases of mouth cancer are identified annually, mainly by dentists. Fourteen hundred of these cases are fatal. Early diagnosis gives the best chance so, particularly in smokers, regular dental checks can save lives.

Chemicals, heat and cancer

Heat from the smoke contributes to the damage, but the chemicals from the tobacco play a key role. There is a high incidence of mouth, throat and nose cancer in users of smokeless tobacco (chewers, snuff dippers and snorters) and, in smokers, cancer often begins in the lowest parts of the mouth where the smoky saliva tends to pool but the heat does not have much access. In pipe smokers, cancer can develop where the end of the pipe stem habitually rests, which is where the heat and chemicals are most concentrated.

Cancer follows the chemicals

In some pipe and cigar smokers, mouth cancer is more common than in cigarette smokers. However, there is a distinction between those who have only ever smoked pipes or cigars, who tend not to inhale, and those who have taken to pipe or cigar smoking after giving up cigarettes. Nowadays, about three quarters of pipe and cigar smokers are ex-cigarette smokers, and they tend to inhale their smoke, diverting more of the carcinogens from mouth to lungs. Unlike the non-inhalers, they suffer the same kind and degree of disease as cigarette smokers, sometimes more.

In general, if smoke is inhaled, the carcinogens and other constituents of smoke go to the lungs. If the smoke is not inhaled but held in the mouth, or if chewing tobacco or dipping snuff is used, the chemicals stay some time in the mouth, tending to pool in the low bits, before being swallowed. If the smoke is held in the mouth between sips of drink or bites of food, the carcinogens and other chemicals will go rather sooner to the digestive system.

Heat and cancer

Probably the highest rates of mouth cancer in the world are suffered by a small group of native South Americans whose habitual method of smoking their hand-made cigars is to have the burning end inside the mouth: a clear indication, if one were needed, that heat plays a part in smokers' mouth cancer.

A similar effect of heat in facilitating cancer has been seen in one part of China, where cancer of the oesophagus (food pipe) was unusually high. The big difference in this local population was their habit of swallowing their food extremely hot. A typical meal might be a bowl of noodles in a thin soup and this is almost drunk from the bowl, swallowing quickly before the mouth gets too burned. The constant heat damage to the lining of the oesophagus may, for example, allow easier access to viruses which can cause cancer but, whatever the mechanism, education into eating food cooler has been effective in reducing the problem in this population.

46

Smoking and drinking

Because alcohol also plays a part in cancer of the mouth and throat, and many heavy smokers in Western countries are also heavy drinkers, it is hard to be precise about the number of deaths from mouth cancer due to smoking alone. Smoking 40 or more cigarettes a day and having four or more alcoholic drinks leads to about 35 times as many deaths from mouth and throat cancer as compared with non-smokers who are light drinkers. Heavy smoking alone probably carries a 20–30 fold risk but the risk is less for lighter smokers.

Cancer treatment: a luxury for the wealthy

The worldwide incidence of tobacco-related mouth, throat and oesophageal cancers is somewhat different from that in Western countries, and so is the treatment and outcome.

Such cancers currently account for about 2.4% of the roughly 3 million deaths a year from tobacco use worldwide. The total is set to rise as today's smokers become tomorrow's health statistics, but the proportion due to this range of cancers will depend on how tobacco is consumed. In parts of South East Asia and India, tobacco chewing is becoming very common, and mouth, throat and oesophageal cancers are increasing.

In advanced countries, treatment, though severe, is often successful in saving life. A recent medical conference in Tokyo was devoted to the treatment of head and neck cancers. After removal of parts of the mouth or throat, reconstructive surgery and tissue grafting, using sections of the patient's small intestine, is possible. These are both for cosmetic reasons and to restore some function, and there are some highly sophisticated techniques available.

That tobacco and alcohol use was the major cause of these cancers was accepted with resignation by the specialists discussing how best to treat them, but one delegate from Bombay (these cancers account for 35% of cancers in India) described reconstructive surgery as a 'daunting task' due to the profound prevalence of the disease and shortage of specialist surgeons. For many people in the poorest countries, treatment will simply be unavailable or unaffordable.

Summary of effects of smoking on the respiratory system

From the mouth, smoke passes down the throat and into the lungs via the bronchi. Smoking damages these areas and aids the spread of respiratory infections.

Mouth

Three quarters of deaths from mouth/throat cancer are caused by smoking. (Smokeless tobacco use increases the risk)

Coughs and colds

Respiratory infections spread to others by germs riding on exhaled smoke

Fewer antibodies in mucus so more infections (coughs and colds)

Bronchitis

Airway linings irritable, so more coughing

More and thicker mucus produced

System for removing it paralysed, leading to coughing

Emphysema

Destruction of lung tissue caused by:
- direct damage to lung tissue
- lung defence system going wrong, digesting lung tissue
- mechanical damage due to coughing

Lung cancer

More than 90% of cases caused by tobacco smoke

Causes more deaths than any other cancer, in men and in women

Blood vessels, heart and blood

Chemicals from smoke in the lungs have rapid access to the blood, and they cause immediate damage just as they do in the lungs. The damage can lead to circulatory failure, either because vessels get blocked or because they burst. Most heart attacks are caused by blocked vessels, and strokes are caused by either.

Blood vessels

Blood vessel walls are damaged by smoke chemicals.

The walls of all but the smallest vessels are muscular, allowing the blood flow through the vessel to be controlled. Lining the inside of vessels is a layer of smooth 'non-stick' cells called the endothelium. Blood won't clot on healthy endothelium, but as soon as there is any injury and the blood touches the muscle lying behind the endothelium, clotting is triggered – part of the normal control of bleeding from wounds.

The cells of the endothelium produce, amongst other things, nitric oxide. This passes into the vessel wall and keeps the muscle relaxed and the vessel open. When the nitric oxide supply is reduced, the vessel narrows, and if it fails altogether, for instance when a vessel is injured, the vessel goes into spasm, closing down almost completely – another part of the normal control of bleeding from wounds. Useful as this is in injury, if it happens inappropriately, for example in a vessel whose lining but not wall has been damaged, it can be dangerous.

Smoke chemicals in blood, particularly the irritants and oxidants, directly damage the endothelium, opening up tiny spaces between the cells and exposing the muscle. This has been seen directly, in experiments with smokers' blood. When the liquid part of their blood is passed over healthy endothelium, the damage is visible under a microscope.

Phagocytes behaving badly again

As well as damaging the endothelium directly, the smoke chemicals in blood also make the phagocytes angry.

This has also been seen directly, in experiments looking closely at blood flow in living vessels. Normally, the blood cells don't touch the vessel walls. They glide along, separated from the wall by a thin layer of plasma, the liquid part of blood. Fifteen minutes after a cigarette, however, phagocytes are clinging to the walls, singly and in clumps, some with sticky platelets clinging to them. Platelets becoming sticky are the first stage of a blood clot, and the phagocytes are angered by the smoke chemicals.

Space invaders

As soon as spaces open up in the endothelium, several things happen. Components of blood including phagocytes can invade the vessel wall, blood begins to clot on the exposed muscle, and the endothelium tries to heal itself by growing over the damaged area. These are the first steps to blockage of the vessel.

Hardening of the arteries

Generalized damage to the vessel wall occurs to us all as we age; the arterial walls in particular become thicker and stiffer. Nowadays, arterial wall thickness can be measured by ultrasound, a patient-friendly and non-invasive technique. Thickening of the arteries implies hardening of the arteries, and is a reliable predictor of death from cardiovascular disease.

In smokers, thickening progresses 50% faster than in non-smokers. For ex-smokers not exposed to passive smoking the figure is still 25%, suggesting that some of the damage caused by smoking is not halted by quitting.

One possible explanation involves the tiny blood vessels which run through the muscle of the arterial walls. Although muscle close to the endothelium can get its oxygen directly from the passing blood, in thick-walled arteries the outer layers of muscle are too distant for this to be a sufficient supply. The vessels which serve the outer layers of muscle are called *vasa vasorum* (vessels of the vessels), and they are to the arteries what the coronaries are to the heart. Being tiny, they are easily blocked, and if they do become blocked then the vessel wall will inevitably suffer.

Bursting arteries

As well as becoming thicker and stiffer, arteries get weaker. Arteries need to be strong and elastic to cope with the blood pressure pulse, and when they stiffen, they are more likely to burst. A burst vessel in the brain can cause temporary or permanent loss of brain function, otherwise known as a stroke, and in severe cases a burst is fatal.

The other main risk of death comes from a burst in the aorta, the main artery coming out of the left side of the heart. As all the blood in the body is pumped through the aorta in about a minute and a half, less during exercise, death is almost certain if the aorta bursts. For every twelve people dying this way, eleven are either smokers or ex-smokers.

Blockage

Vessels can be blocked when the muscles in the vessel wall contract, or by blood clots or lumps in the wall. Damaged endothelium can lead to constriction of the muscle in the vessel wall. A clot may block the vessel where it occurs, or it can break free and cause a blockage downstream. Invasion of the wall can lead, over time, to atheroma or atherosclerotic plaques, raised lumpy patches full of phagocytes, fat and scar tissue. A fatty diet can also lead to atheroma, so smoking is not the only culprit. Sometimes the plaque forms a crusty top which can break away, causing a blockage where it jams in a narrower vessel downstream.

Effects of blocked vessels

This depends on which vessel is blocked. In the brain, the result is a stroke.

A common site of blocked vessels in smokers is the legs, with many small arteries becoming blocked. Initially, the sufferer feels pain on walking, due to the shortage of oxygen. Treatment includes drugs to dilate the blood vessels and grafting to bypass major blockages, but as the condition advances gangrene can set in and the only recourse then is amputation.

In England and Wales, 29 legs a week are amputated, most of these from smokers. However, amputation is the treatment of last resort and far more smokers live out their days in a wheelchair, or severely restricted in their movement.

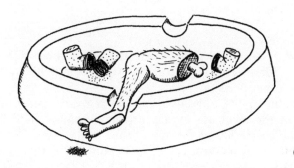

Gangrene

Creeping up again . . .

The destruction of the circulation is not something that happens suddenly when a smoker gets old – it is creeping up with every cigarette smoked. Blood vessel damage and the beginnings of blockage occur long before any symptoms appear. Recent evidence suggests that it occurs at a low level of exposure to smoke, because passive smokers are little better off than hardened smokers.

Phagocytes behaving better

When not upset by smoke, phagocytes are great repairers and cleaners. They eat up debris left after injury, and this includes blood clots. Left to get on with their work, they will deal with small clots and debris, reducing the risk of permanent blockage of blood vessels, but what they can achieve is limited by the next cigarette.

Blood pressure and the endothelium

The endothelium is more than just a non-stick lining. It plays a crucial role in controlling blood pressure.

Blood can be diverted to where it is needed in the body, such as the leg muscles when running, by opening up some vessels and squeezing down others. However, if all vessels are squeezed down then the heart has to pump much harder to get the blood to flow, and the blood pressure rises. A healthy person has fairly relaxed vessels, allowing a moderate blood pressure. Vessels are kept relaxed by the endothelium constantly releasing nitric oxide into the vessel wall muscle. When the endothelium is disrupted by hostile smoke chemicals in the blood, this mechanism is under threat.

Overall, the damage done is a balance between the injury caused by the smoke chemicals and the body's efforts to repair it before the next cigarette.

Heart

The heart is a special case because it is far more vulnerable to blockage of its vessels – the coronaries, which supply the heart muscle – than are other parts of the body.

The vulnerability is for two reasons: firstly, the heart never stops moving, so the mechanical wear on the coronaries adds to smoke damage, and secondly, blood cannot flow in the coronaries when the heart muscle is at its most contracted. This means that the blood in the coronaries sits still for part of each heartbeat, during which time most of the oxygen is extracted from it. When the heart needs more oxygen to work harder, it can't get any more from the blood that is there so it must get more blood to flow.

Furthermore, smoking has an immediate and bad effect of on the coronary circulation. Modern medical techniques allow doctors to watch a television picture of the coronary arteries in awake patients and to measure the blood flow through them, at the same time as recording other things such as pulse rate and blood pressure. One study investigating chest pain in smokers described observations involving 24 patients.

Five minutes after patients had smoked a cigarette, both pulse rate and blood pressure had risen (the expected response to nicotine), meaning that the heart was working faster and harder and so needed more oxygen. Nevertheless, flow through the coronary vessels was reduced (nicotine causes blood vessels, including the coronaries, to constrict), cutting down the oxygen supply. Things were back to baseline after about 30 minutes.

In one patient, a section of coronary artery suddenly narrowed dramatically. It had gone into spasm following the cigarette. This could well have been the start of a heart attack, but fortunately for the patient, immediate drug treatment relaxed the vessel.

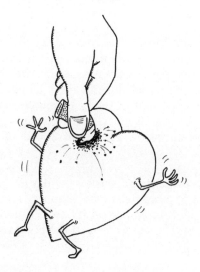

Heart attack

Heart attack and angina

Any blockage or inability to open up the vessels restricts the blood flow, and when a patch of heart muscle is starved of oxygen, a heart attack can result. If the blockage is insufficient to cause an outright heart attack, pain and heaviness is felt, usually in the chest or upper left arm. This is called angina pectoris, frequently shortened to angina; it is the familiar pain of any over-used muscle, but the heart muscle cannot stop to rest and angina must be taken seriously. It is a warning of the possibility of a heart attack if matters get worse.

Blood

Smoking damages the blood in ways which compound the damage to the blood vessels.

Smoke chemicals interfere with the clotting mechanism, making clotting more easily triggered. The blood is also thicker because it has extra red cells; these are produced in an attempt to compensate for the red cells being clogged with carbon monoxide. The thicker blood is harder to pump and more sluggish, so it puts extra strain on the heart. Blood which is flowing slowly, for whatever reason, also clots more readily than fast-flowing blood.

Furthermore, the blood is being used to distribute the smoke chemicals to all parts of the body. Many cancers are smoking-related, and the carcinogens are delivered by the blood.

Carbon monoxide

Carbon monoxide cuts down the amount of oxygen the blood can carry. Too high a concentration of carbon monoxide is lethal; smoking alone cannot supply a lethal dose, but someone smoking 40 cigarettes a day has about 20% of the lethal dose in their blood. The reduction in available oxygen is important to the heart muscle, to the endothelium and to the leg muscles of someone already showing signs of trouble. The brain, too, becomes sluggish when oxygen is in short supply.

Hydrogen cyanide

Hydrogen cyanide prevents cells using the oxygen which is available. Whilst not present in cigarette smoke in quantities sufficient to make more than a marginal difference on its own, it adds to the effect of carbon monoxide in denying oxygen to the body tissues.

Nicotine

As well as being the main cause of the addictiveness of tobacco products, nicotine acts on the blood vessels and heart, raising both blood pressure and heart rate. For a heart already struggling with a decreased oxygen supply, this adds to the trouble.

The first cigarette of the day has a greater effect in this regard than do subsequent ones, a phenomenon known as 'acute tolerance', because the body adapts to the presence of nicotine. The period overnight without smoking restores the response.

Acute tolerance to the effect of nicotine on blood pressure and heart rate helps account for an anomaly long recognized in smokers: although nicotine raises the blood pressure, smokers as a group apparently do not suffer from such high blood pressure as expected. It cannot account fully, though; other factors must be at work.

Numerical risks of cardiovascular disease for smokers

Roughly seven times as many smokers die of heart disease as die of lung cancer. Adding cerebrovascular disease (strokes caused by blockage or bursting of blood vessels in the brain) raises this figure to ten times.

Lung cancer is far more famous as a killer of smokers because very little else causes lung cancer, making it the first of the smoking-induced killer diseases to be recognized. The relative risk to smokers over non-smokers of cardiovascular disease, two to three times, reflects the fact that other things also cause cardiovascular disease, which is why it was overlooked for some time as being a consequence of smoking. Relative risks are very high in younger smokers: in men under 45, 80% of heart attacks are due to smoking, but with increasing age, other risks catch up.

However, recent evidence on the thickening of arterial walls in response to quite modest levels of passive smoking puts a question mark over the size of the risk of cardiovascular disease from smoking. If some of the non-smokers used to gauge the smokers by were passive smokers, the real risk could be somewhat greater than the two to three times currently quoted.

Summary of effects of smoking on the circulatory system

Blood takes up smoke chemicals from the lungs and distributes them all over the body. In transit they damage the blood itself, the blood vessels and the heart.

Blood

Thicker, so harder to pump
More prone to clot and block vessels
Delivers less oxygen
Toxic to vessel linings (endothelium)

Blood vessels

Linings damaged: can lead to blockage by constriction, clots and atheroma
Walls stiffened and weakened: can burst

Heart

Driven by nicotine to work harder and faster
Extra effort needed to pump thicker blood through damaged vessels
Decreased oxygen supply to heart muscle: risk of heart attack
High risk of blockage in coronary vessels: heart attack

CHAPTER 6
Other parts of the body

Beyond the lungs and the cardiovascular system, it is increasingly difficult to be precise about how smoking is doing the damage. Much of the hard information available is in terms of relative rates of disease in smokers and non-smokers. The list below reflects that evidence, but it is almost certainly not a complete catalogue of the health consequences of smoking.

Kidneys	Skin
Bladder	Wound healing
Digestive system	Reproductive systems
Pancreas	Cervical cancer
Liver	Osteoporosis
Eyes	

In addition, it has been suggested that smoking has beneficial effects in some conditions. The three best-known are ulcerative colitis, Alzheimer's disease and Parkinson's disease.

Kidneys

The kidneys take about 20% of the blood coming out of the left side of the heart and their job is to clean it. As the blood flows through the kidneys, water and waste, including cotinine and nicotine-N-oxide, break-down products of nicotine, are filtered off through the blood vessel walls and flow down tubes to the bladder, where they may be stored for some time.

The practical details are more complex. Blood entering the kidney is divided up into vast numbers of tiny vessels, so the blood is 'spread out' over a huge area of the specialized vessel wall through which the waste is filtered. The tiny tubes which collect the waste are arranged in a beautiful structure which enables the kidneys to concentrate the urine when the body is short of water as well as get rid of it when there is an excess.

This means that the kidneys are responsible for controlling the blood volume. Given that the blood has to fit into a roughly fixed space, some of which is bounded by elastic arteries, if the volume goes too high the blood pressure rises and if it drops too low then the pressure cannot be kept high enough.

Water is just one of many things whose exit from the body is tightly regulated by the kidneys. By controlling how much acidic and alkaline matter goes into urine, the kidneys are also part of the system for keeping the body at neutral acidity. Other aspects of body chemistry, for example keeping conditions right for the electrical activity of nerves and muscles, are also influenced by the kidneys.

The control is achieved by minute and intricate local regulation of blood flow and pressure, through the action of nerves as well as hormones (chemical messengers) but also by some active pumping of selected substances across the membranes. Anything which upsets the workings of the kidneys has serious consequences for the whole person.

Normally, we can get by quite happily on one kidney; generous donors give one of their healthy kidneys to save the life of someone, often a close relative, in mortal need of a transplant. In fact, one good kidney can be better than one good one and one not working properly. For example, a blood clot or other debris (and smokers have an increased risk of both these) restricting the blood supply to one kidney can cause it to take totally inappropriate action, releasing hormones into the blood which push up the blood pressure. This won't clear the blockage, puts extra strain on the heart and hastens arterial problems all over the body.

On a finer scale, the membranes of the kidney are just as vulnerable to hostile chemicals from the smoke as are the lungs and the rest of the blood vessels, and kidney damage can result. We can get along with reduced kidney function, just as with reduced lung function, for a long time before the trouble surfaces, unless a sudden increase in demand shows how functionally reduced the kidneys have become.

Finally, kidney cancer has grabbed far fewer headlines than lung cancer but it, too, is smoking-related.

Bladder

The urine collects in the bladder and can be stored there for hours, so anything in it has plenty of time to get to work on the tissues of the bladder. It is a tough, watertight holding tank but it is made of living tissue and is susceptible to cancer. Cancer of the bladder is strongly associated both with smoking and with the quantities smoked.

Digestive system

Tobacco products have two ways of getting into the digestive system, either swallowed from the mouth or coughed up from the lungs and bronchi into the back of the throat and then swallowed. Either way, the inner surface of the digestive system gets a heavy exposure in addition to what is blood-borne to its tissues.

Cancers of the oesophagus (gullet, food pipe) and stomach are both strongly associated with smoking and the quantities smoked, though cancer of the colon, which is towards the end of the intestine, is only weakly linked to smoking, if at all. However, at the final stage of the intestine, the rectum, which is where the food waste (faeces) is held before excretion, cancer is once more strongly smoking-related; a situation similar to that in the bladder.

A common problem in the stomach and duodenum (the bit of the intestine immediately after the stomach) is ulcers. In these areas, they are called peptic ulcers. An ulcer is an area of damaged tissue that won't heal; it is red and raw, painful, sometimes swollen, sometimes sunken into the tissue, and it carries the danger of unseen bleeding into the digestive tract which, if unstopped, can add up to serious blood loss. In recent years it has emerged that at the root of most peptic ulcers is a bacterium, *helicobacter pylori*, which can be successfully killed off by a course of antibiotics and other drugs, following which the ulcer heals.

While smoking clearly is not the source of *h. pylori*, it does increase the risk of ulcer development, possibly by making it easier for germs to invade tissues. Smoking also makes existing ulcers worse and slows down the healing. Heavy smokers are at greater risk of ulcers than light ones, and all smokers are at greater risk than non-smokers.

Pancreas

The pancreas lies just below the stomach and secretes enzymes used by the digestive system for breaking down food. It also secretes two well-known hormones, insulin and glucagon, which regulate blood sugar levels. (Failure of this regulation is the disease diabetes.) Cancer of the pancreas is difficult to treat and it, too, is strongly linked to smoking, being around three times as common in heavy smokers as in non-smokers.

Liver

The liver is one of the few organs apparently not at great risk from smoking. It is the largest glandular organ and sits on the right at the top of the abdomen, just below the diaphragm. It is concerned with the processing of nutrients in the blood (alcohol and nicotine are both broken down in the liver), as well as the storage of some vitamins and minerals. It has, quite literally, hundreds of individual jobs to do and, in relation to smoking, is an interesting example of the care needed in interpreting statistics.

Cancer of the liver is, like cancer of the pancreas, very hard to treat but its incidence is not, or is only weakly, correlated with smoking (results of different studies vary on this question, though none claim a huge correlation). However, cirrhosis of the liver correlates very strongly indeed with smoking. There is very little rationale for this except the indisputable fact that many heavy smokers are also heavy drinkers, suggesting that it is the drink, not the smoke, doing the damage.

Eyes

Macular degeneration used to be rare, but it is now one of the commoner causes of blindness in the elderly. The macula is the part of the eye where the highest density of light-sensitive nerve cells is found and through which all detailed vision passes. To get an idea of the effect of macular degeneration, shut one eye and hold a finger up close to the other, so close that it just about touches the eyelashes. As long as it remains in the centre of what you can see, it is blocking out most of the view falling on the macula. The bits around the edge which you can see are only vague and you cannot, for example, read any print visible (if you can, you have moved your eye to look round the edge of your finger).

Macular degeneration is a disease predominantly of the elderly. Several studies have now shown that it is more common in smokers than in non-smokers: typically, smoking more than 20 a day increases the risk by 2.5 times. It is one of the few risks which does not decrease after quitting.

Skin

It's true, smoking does make you look old and wrinkly. Youthful skin is plump and smooth but it gets thinner as it ages. Smoking thins and ages it faster and a perfectly good candidate for the mechanism is poor blood supply. Nicotine constricts the vessels going to the skin and, unlike the rest of the vessels in the body, they do not display acute tolerance: constriction is directly related to the quantity of nicotine in the blood. In addition, they are subject to the same damage from atheroma as are other vessels.

Psoriasis is also more common in smokers than non-smokers. It is a socially disabling condition in which patches of the skin, including on the face, are raised, red and scaly. It tends to last for a long time and one study concludes that about a quarter of all cases could be triggered by smoking.

Wound healing

Healing of any wound depends on the damaged tissues being removed and new ones growing in the right places and, in fact, smokers' wounds tend to take longer to heal. One reason is that their inflammatory phagocytes, which carry out many of the repairs, are made angry by the smoke chemicals. Angry inflammatory phagocytes do a poor repair job and can be destructive, as in the lungs.

Another reason is that, to heal properly, wounds need a very good blood supply bringing in all the materials used in the repair. With blood supply to the skin restricted by the action of nicotine, oxygen limited by carbon monoxide and hydrogen cyanide, sluggish blood and extra clots to be cleared away, repairs are slow. The irritant components of tobacco smoke also get in the way of healing.

Reproductive systems

Even soot causes cancer. The first environmentally- (though not tobacco-) related cancer recorded was in 1775 when Dr Percival Pott noticed a high incidence of cancer of the scrotum in chimney sweeps. The soot lodged in the wrinkles of the skin and few sweeps would have had the benefit of warm water for washing.

Both men and women suffer reduced fertility as a result of smoking. Smoking is emphatically not a reliable contraceptive in the majority of people, but for some less fertile couples it can prevent conception. Many fertility clinics now consider quitting as an essential prerequisite to any treatment.

In male smokers, both the sperm density and the sperm quality are adversely affected. Sperm are more sluggish, less determined swimmers. Cotinine, the main break-down product of nicotine, is thought to be at least partly responsible, as are disturbed hormone levels, but there is a lot of detail we don't yet know about the damage to sperm.

A bit of a let-down . . .

Virility is under another threat, too. Impotence is more common among smokers and ex-smokers than among non-smokers, and under certain conditions a couple of cigarettes or even injected nicotine can prevent erection. A press release has announced recent research (publication August 1998) showing that smoking shrinks the penis. Apparently the small arteries which enable erection become damaged.

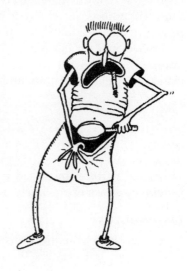

Erection happens when the arteries open up to allow blood at arterial pressure to inflate the penis. The mechanism relies on the potential inflow of blood being greater than the outflow via the veins, which are constricted. When the inflow gets restricted, either by nicotine or permanently by damage to the arterial walls, it can be insufficient to maintain a full erection, leaving smokers' penises smaller and limper.

Female smokers trying to conceive take longer to do so than non-smokers, and those undertaking in vitro fertilization have a 50% lower pregnancy rate than do non-smokers. Ovaries of women exposed to smoke (passive as well as active smokers) contain some of the harmful chemicals from smoke; again, more knowledge is needed.

Smoking also increases the risk of an ectopic pregnancy (the embryo implanting outside the womb) and evidence is gathering that smoking during pregnancy can even, by disturbing the mother's hormonal balance, affect the reproductive system of the developing child.

In addition, smoking in conjunction with the use of oestrogen-containing oral contraceptives multiplies by ten the risk of cardiovascular disease in young women; over 45, the risk is even higher. Oestrogen-containing oral contraceptives are the most commonly-used kind. They are known as the 'combined' pill because they combine the female hormones oestrogen and progestogen. The mini-pill, which relies on progestogen alone, has a much lower risk in conjunction with smoking, but because delaying taking it for only a few hours can make it ineffective it is not the contraceptive of choice for most women.

Smoking also makes the menopause come a year or two earlier, and both this and the strong interaction with oestrogen-based contraceptives indicates that smoking interferes with female hormones. The increased waist-to-hip ratio in smokers argues the same thing and decreased female fertility, too, is consistent; one possibility is a damaged blood supply to the ovaries, which themselves release hormones. Nicotine certainly interferes with the brain's control of the master hormone-releasing site, the pituitary gland, just below the brain and behind the bridge of the nose.

Cervical cancer

Smoking can increase by a factor of four the risk of developing cervical cancer. The risk increases with the quantity smoked and the duration of smoking. Evidence demonstrating that smoking is associated with an increased risk of cervical cancer is supported by genetic evidence of the likely mechanism.

Osteoporosis

Osteoporosis is a loss of density in bones, affecting predominantly post-menopausal women, though it can occur in men and younger women. It is linked to the decrease in oestrogen which happens at the menopause, and the affected bones are weaker and more brittle, so prone to fracture. Wrists, hips and the spine seem to be the most vulnerable. Smokers are at greater risk of osteoporosis, both because the menopause comes a couple of years early and because smokers seem to suffer a greater decrease in oestrogen than do non-smokers. Osteoporosis can be induced in other ways: heavy metal and other trace elements in tobacco smoke accumulate in bone and could trigger osteoporosis and other disorders of mineral metabolism.

Positive effects of smoking?

With all the ill effects of smoking, it is particularly interesting to know whether there are any good effects beyond the subjective pleasure experienced by smokers. The three best-known candidates are the effects of smoking on ulcerative colitis, Alzheimer's disease and Parkinson's disease.

Ulcerative colitis

This is a condition in which parts of the colon and rectum become inflamed and painful, with ulcers developing. Diarrhoea is a common complication and, at best, the condition is socially difficult. The cause is as yet unknown but it is largely a disease of non-smokers, and anecdotal evidence suggests that smoking improves symptoms. Studies designed to investigate this evidence showed that nicotine patches, in addition to normal medication for the condition, did improve matters.

That nicotine should have an effect on the gut is no surprise. In the embryo, the gut and brain develop from the same group of cells, and many substances active in the brain also have effects in the gut. The effect of nicotine on ulcerative colitis could be an important clue in gaining a better understanding of the condition.

Alzheimer's disease

This is a degenerative brain disease in which, post mortem, the brain shows extreme signs of normal ageing and has characteristic histological features including loss of brain tissue in specific areas. Sufferers display loss of memory, confusion and disorientation. Recent ideas include the possibility that the damage could be due, at least in part, to damage to blood vessels supplying the area.

Alzheimer's disease was originally defined as pre-senile dementia, and distinguished from senile dementia by its onset before the age of 60. However, it is now clear that the disease processes are the same, and the term Alzheimer's is used irrespective of the age of onset. There is some degree of inherited tendency.

It has been suggested, and seized on by the tobacco lobby, that smoking reduces the chances of suffering from Alzheimer's disease. The most obvious pitfall when simply comparing the disease in smokers and non-smokers is that smokers, who have shorter lives than non-smokers, avoid Alzheimer's disease by dying before succumbing to it. Some early studies showing that smokers had a lower risk were invalid because they excluded patients with heart disease or strokes, which would have excluded more smokers than non-smokers. A large recent study, designed to eliminate the earlier confounding factors, found that smoking more than doubles the risk of developing Alzheimer's disease. For carriers of a particular gene, the risk was increased almost fivefold by smoking.

It has also been suggested that nicotine improves symptoms for people already suffering from Alzheimer's disease. Nicotine is known to act on many systems in the brain, including some of those damaged in the course of the disease, so there is a rationale for such an effect to exist. However, the evidence so far purporting to show that nicotine or smoking can improve matters in the far more complex situation in the living brain is weak.

If smoking does alleviate the symptoms, then this indicates a way forward in looking for more effective treatments, possibly based on nicotine, rather than constituting a recommendation to smoke. What is absolutely clear now is that smoking does not protect against developing Alzheimer's disease; indeed, it more than doubles the risk.

Parkinson's disease

This is another disease of the brain, though it is confined to a well-known and well-studied part of the brain. It tends to affect men more than women, and predominantly older people, though there is an early onset form of the disease.

Its most visible effects are muscular rigidity and muscular tremor or shaking. The tremor is most noticeable in the hands, where it can become so severe that writing and even holding a cup are impossible, and in the legs, making walking difficult. Rigidity is most often obvious in the face, where a lack of any expression is most disconcerting to observers. Another effect is that speech is slow and the first word can be disturbingly delayed. A hidden distress to the sufferer is the effect this has on other people, who can assume, totally wrongly, that the lack of response indicates lack of feeling or thought. The thoughts are all there but the facial and vocal muscles which signal them can't be driven properly.

A curious additional symptom of Parkinson's disease is a disordered sense of smell, and current ideas of the cause of Parkinson's include some agent, possibly a virus, travelling up the nose and into the brain via the olfactory (sense of smell) nerve.

Superficially, smoking would appear to reduce the risk of dying of Parkinson's disease but the picture is complicated by the fact that the symptoms of the disease make smoking difficult, converting some sufferers from smokers to ex-smokers. The argument about smoking killing people off before Parkinson's sets in could also be a valid criticism of some studies.

Leaving aside the question of whether smoking can protect against contracting Parkinson's disease, nicotine is known to act on the part of the brain which is affected, and smoking does appear to be able to transiently alleviate symptoms of some forms of Parkinson's disease; indeed, this effect was first demonstrated in 1926. For instance, a cigarette can reduce tremor sufficiently to allow the sufferer to write a letter or complete some other task. It probably does so by delivering nicotine to the affected part of the brain, which it stimulates. However, the effect only lasts for about half an hour and a second cigarette, as the first one wears off, is less effective (exactly the same as the effect of the first and then the second cigarette of the day on the blood pressure). Nicotine chewing gum also works, though less well, possibly because of the slower uptake and access to the brain.

As with Alzheimer's disease, the authors of studies all point out that any benefits of smoking in alleviating Parkinson's disease are far outweighed by its dangers. However, for someone suffering uncontrollable tremor which can be alleviated by a cigarette, smoking might seem, even on balance, to be attractive. The nicotine inhalers recently introduced as quitting aids may turn out to be a useful alternative to smoking.

Interestingly, a similar reduction in tremor can be achieved merely by cooling the affected muscles. This can be of practical use for the arm: a few minutes in cold or iced water can reduce the tremor sufficiently to allow a brief period of normal use, until the arm warms up again. Unlike nicotine, the effect is immediately repeatable and is only limited by the individual's enthusiasm for wet and wintry conditions.

Overall effects of smoking

Tobacco roulette

Smoking is overwhelmingly bad for the body, even, it is now clear, in the small quantities associated with passive smoking. Many diseases, including cancers, are encouraged by smoking or smokeless tobacco. The risk of some cancers and other diseases is dramatically increased by these products.

Nicotine may have some benefits for people suffering from Parkinson's disease or ulcerative colitis, and possibly even Alzheimer's disease, but smoking more than doubles the risk of developing Alzheimer's disease. No-one is suggesting that smoking is appropriate in these conditions, only that nicotine may be beneficial.

One smoker in two will die prematurely of a smoking related disease, with one in four who began as a teenager losing 20–25 years of life. Most smokers will suffer excess ill health as a result of smoking, and all smokers risk making others ill, or even killing them, with their smoke.

CHAPTER 7
Health professionals

Doctors as a group were the first great quitters

People in the healthcare professions see smokers all the time, and are well aware of the effects of smoking. Indeed, doctors as a group were the first great quitters, when the news about smoking and lung cancer was published.

GPs see the day-to-day problems when they have surfaced, anaesthetists deal most closely with the immediate consequences of smoking and dentists see in detail what smoking, as well as snuff dipping and tobacco chewing, does to the mouth.

GP: smoking, the individual and the family

"Smoking is an enormous part of my responsibility as a GP. It is by far the greatest avoidable cause of ill-health, accounting for about 30% of all cancers, most chronic obstructive lung disease," (bronchitis and emphysema) "plenty of cardiovascular disease and lots more.

A touchy subject

"You need to exercise tact on the subject of smoking when dealing with some patients. It's a touchy subject; if mum comes in with an infant with a wheezy chest, and you ask her if she or dad smokes, it's like suggesting that they aren't caring for their child properly. Lots of ear infections, asthma and chest infections in children are due to smokers in the home, but it's a difficult one to approach without upsetting people, and once you've upset them, you can't help them.

"Overall, the most difficult patients to help are the hardened smokers. They look away when smoking is mentioned and they're beyond hearing advice, so there's little which can be done for them except treating the health problems as they arise.

Becoming parents

"We routinely ask expectant mums about smoking; before they're pregnant, if possible. Smoking in pregnancy increases the chance of miscarriage, growth retardation in the womb and cot death, and we encourage them to think very heavily about smoking. Smoking by the father is not an issue we address at present, though it ought to be, given the recent findings on childhood cancers and smoking by dads around the time of conception. We tend not to see the dads at this stage, anyhow; the mums come along on their own and the dads generally only appear around the time of the birth.

Invisible teenagers

"The biggest problem for us in trying to reduce the number of smokers is the teenagers. They're pretty healthy at this stage in their lives, so we don't see them, which means we don't get a chance to discuss their smoking habit, though we do try to talk to teenage girls when they come for contraception. Up to about 10 or 11, they're all keenly anti-smoking, but by the time they're 13 or so, they're established smokers. Of course, there's millions spent advertising to them.

Help for quitters

"We did run a special clinic for quitters at one stage, but attendance rates were poor. I prefer to see people on a one-to-one basis, because this seems to be more successful. What I do is to review them weekly for the first four weeks. I know it seems wasteful to use regular surgery time for this, but I think it's worthwhile; many of my patients wouldn't be here if they weren't smokers. Round here, we buy patients their first week's nicotine replacement out of money from a charitable fund, and I think some other GPs do similar things.

"When someone manages to quit, the results are tremendous! They get a dramatic health improvement, and it's a huge boost to their self-esteem. Some of them find it's not so difficult as they thought it was going to be, and of course they're far better off financially. Yes, we get quite a lot of success with quitters."

Anaesthetist: respiration, circulation and smoking

Every smoker going into hospital for surgery is advised to stop smoking. A general anaesthetic is one circumstance in which smoking is likely to send the blood pressure sky high – the anaesthetist's, not the smoker's.

Anaesthetists have to work daily with the practical effects of smoking on the airways, lungs and circulation, and a chat with an anaesthetist reveals that absolutely all smokers are adversely affected.

What do anaesthetists do?

Anaesthetists do more than put the patient to sleep while the surgeon gets on with the business and then wake them up again afterwards. For much surgery under general anaesthesia, the patient is sufficiently paralysed to prevent involuntary movement, so breathing has to be assisted. It is the anaesthetist's job to attend to the pumping of air and anaesthetic gases in and out of the patient's lungs, making sure that the patient stays unconscious and the blood stays sufficiently oxygenated to maintain life and health.

By the use of a wide range of drugs, the anaesthetist will also control the patient's pulse rate and blood pressure. For a few surgical procedures, a fairly low blood pressure is useful because it decreases bleeding. On top of this maintenance function, the anaesthetist has to be ready for every imaginable emergency: adverse reactions to drugs or manipulations, for example.

All those things which the patient's brain normally keeps under perfect subconscious control – depth and rate of breathing, pulse rate and blood pressure, even temperature – are now managed by the anaesthetist and there is very little they don't know back to front, inside out and upside down about the way patients' hearts and lungs perform.

For some lighter surgical procedures, for example the simpler

69

varicose vein operations, some eye surgery and some minor gynecological jobs, it is not necessary to paralyze the patient, who thus breathes the anaesthetic gases through a special mask. This has a lot of advantages for patient and medics, but with smokers there are possible problems.

Problems presented by smokers

One anaesthetist gave the following account of working on smokers:

"Smokers present several problems for anaesthetists, apart from overt disease. The first problem is that their airways are very irritable, so except when paralysed the patient is very prone to coughing and spluttering, particularly when they're coming round. Sometimes they get a spasm of the larynx, which constricts enough for them to turn blue, at which point you judge whether to grab the oxygen mask to get them through to consciousness (when the coughing subsides a bit) or, in a really serious case, reparalyze them, put the tube back and pump them for a bit and pray for better luck next time.

"When you're working with a patient who is not paralysed, smokers can get into trouble at any moment. The irritability of the airways means they can cough and splutter under light anaesthesia and even start wheezing – a bit like an asthma attack – during surgery, so you have to be prepared to intervene if necessary.

"Ideally, smokers should give up 6–8 weeks before surgery, by when the airways will have returned more or less to normal, at least as far as irritability goes. If you can't get them to stop, then you have to do your damnedest to persuade them not to smoke for about 24 hours before surgery – that way, most of the carbon monoxide is gone, which is an enormous help, and the airway irritability is at least down a bit. The patients who sneak off into the toilets for a quick fag shortly before surgery – and there are even some who do it after the pre-med – really are making the anaesthetist's job very hard, what with extremely irritable airways and lots of carbon monoxide.

"In patients who have been smoking for some time, lung function is poor, so getting enough oxygen into the blood is that much harder. The carbon monoxide makes life particularly difficult in these patients. They are also likely to have dickey hearts and bad circulation, neither of which is ideal.

"Then there's the post-op period. Smokers have to cough a lot on coming round to shift the accumulated muck out of the airways, which is rotten for them if the surgery is anywhere in the chest or abdomen – in fact, it's not very nice anywhere. Their wounds tend to take longer to heal, they are more prone to infection and they are at a higher risk of clotting and embolism in the couple of weeks after surgery. Post-operative chest infections are a common, potentially serious, problem in smokers, especially after abdominal surgery.

"Give me a non-smoker every time."

Dentist: tobacco and the mouth

The first part of the body to come into contact with the smoke is the inside of the mouth. Probably the world's greatest experts on bad breath, dentists know whether someone smokes even before looking.

Bad smells, bad teeth

"After the smell, the most obvious signs are cosmetic: yellow staining of the teeth, which get coated in tar and nicotine, but also the effects of bad brushing. Some smokers tend to overbrush while trying to remove the staining caused by the tar. The part of the tooth which is closest to the gum has the thinnest enamel and this can get worn away, leaving the underlying tooth sensitive and vulnerable to decay.

"The other big dental enemy for smokers (for anyone, in fact) is mints – or rather, the sugar in them. Many smokers suck strong mints to overwhelm the smell of tobacco. The sugar is taken up by the bacteria (plaque) which live on the teeth and they ferment it, producing an acid which attacks the teeth, causing decay. With each mint, the acid level in the mouth rises, remaining high enough to attack teeth for about an hour and a half. The acidity falls as the slightly alkaline saliva slowly neutralizes the acid. Sucking a mint at night, when you have decreased salivary flow, can mean that the teeth are under attack for up to six hours.

"Smokers often have poor oral hygiene relative to non-smokers because smoking tends to kill off the normal organisms which live in the mouth. This makes life easier for alternative and often more harmful and smelly life-forms, and these can also encourage gum disease.

Soft tissues – growing a heat-shield

"Just as seriously, the soft tissues in the mouth are directly damaged by smoking. Because they are constantly assaulted by hot and chemically hostile fumes, they do their best to protect themselves by developing a coating of keratin, the substance from which hair and

71

fingernails are made. In effect, the inside of the smoker's mouth is trying to grow a heat-shield.

"In the short term, this is not too much of a problem for most of the lining, but it seriously hampers the salivary glands, and without these our mouths would be dry and our food unchewable. The glands struggle to maintain a channel through the keratin and become inflamed in so doing – hence the characteristic appearance of 'smoker's keratosis', a white thickening of the areas most exposed to the smoke, with the salivary glands showing as red spots.

"In smokers who have a denture, the plate protects the tissues from the smoke and the keratosis starts where the denture plate stops.

Cancer in the mouth

"In most cases the keratosis is a short-term response, clearing up fairly soon (about a month) after the cessation of smoking. However, about 6% of these areas of damage go on to develop into cancer. The damage is due not only to the carcinogenic elements in smoke: the heat works in conjunction with these, damaging the surface so that the chemicals have easier access. Filters tend to cut down the heat of the incoming smoke but people who smoke unfiltered cigarettes and habitually allow them to burn down to their lips suffer keratosis of the lips, with the possibility of cancer developing at the same site.

"These patches of keratosis are also known as leukoplakia (which translates as 'white plates') and they do rarely occur in non-smokers. Smokers carry a higher risk than non-smokers of developing cancer of the mouth and throat, although non-smokers' leukoplakia seem to be more malignant than smokers' leukoplakia – but their comparative rarity means that they are responsible for far fewer cancers of the mouth than are the much more common smokers' leukoplakia.

"Despite the higher malignancy rate in non-smokers' leukoplakia, even these are generally not malignant. The commonest ones are caused by, for example, a rough tooth rubbing perpetually on a cheek, and these tend not to be malignant. In the US, the emphasis is slightly different from that in the UK; smokers' leukoplakia are held to be highly dangerous, though it is hard to say to what extent this is just a difference in attitude and to what extent it is a genuine difference due, for example, to different tobacco use. In any case, dentists in either country will take all leukoplakia, of whatever origin, seriously.

"On an anecdotal rather than a scientific basis, we associate mouth cancer more with pipe smokers than with cigar smokers. It may be no more than a difference in what the mouth is doing when the smoke is around: cigars are often enjoyed at the end of a meal and the high flow rate of saliva (plus the coffee, port or brandy) could help to wash the tar out of the mouth and down the throat. Once the carcinogens are in, they have to go somewhere.

Chewing on the pipe-stem

"Pipe smokers suffer an additional range of problems to do with chewing on the pipe stem: teeth worn down by the pipe stem and pushed out of alignment, and even displaced jaws. Supporting the pipe is the normal state of affairs, so the muscles and joints adapt to it, which means that chewing food, normally the main activity of the jaws, takes second place.

Black hairy tongue

"There is one other condition we see, admittedly rarely, but it is pretty spectacular: 'black hairy tongue'. It occurs in heavy smokers who are also heavy drinkers. The hairy appearance of the tongue is unusually raised taste buds and papillae (the normal lumpy bits on the surface of the tongue) and the black is the tar – not a pretty sight while you're trying to fill a tooth, but then, no smoker's mouth is, really."

CHAPTER 8
Passive smoking

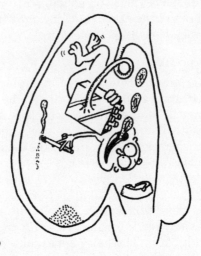

Baby smokes, too

The time has passed when anyone can credibly claim that passive smoking is not harmful. Just like smoking, the damage increases with both the degree of exposure and the youth of the person exposed.

When smokers drag on a cigarette, what they inhale has been through the filter (most people smoke filter-tipped cigarettes now) and is called mainstream smoke. They absorb a fair proportion of it. Side-stream smoke is what curls up from the lit end between drags. It is unfiltered, so more toxic than mainstream smoke, and is the major component of smoke in the room, which is what passive smokers inhale. Of course, active smokers (indoors) are passive smokers too, because they have to breathe between drags.

Most people's idea of passive smoking is sitting in a pub, and the effects of doing this regularly are considerable. However, breathing smoky air is not the only way of being a passive smoker.

Before birth
Far and away the most vulnerable to the effects of someone else's smoking are unborn babies.

Fathers who smoke

If their father smoked around the time of conception, the sperm which brought them half their genes may have been damaged. A UK study published recently concluded that a proportion of childhood cancers could be caused by smoke-damaged sperm, with a 3% increase in the risk when the father smoked fewer than 10 cigarettes a day rising to 31% for 10–20 a day and 42% for more than 20 a day.

A study on children in Shanghai, where smoking is high among men and low among women, was able to calculate individual risks for different kinds of cancer. The risks for children whose fathers smoked at the time of conception, compared with children of non-smoking fathers, were 3.8 times for leukemia, 4.5 for lymphoma, 2.7 for brain tumours and 1.7 averaged over all childhood cancers.

Several studies have shown that smokers produce damaged sperm.

Mothers who smoke

The ovaries of female smokers, including passive smokers, contain hazardous chemicals from smoke. The presence of benzo[a]pyrene, a potent mutagen and carcinogen, in ovaries of women undergoing *in vitro* fertilization suggests the possibility of genetic damage. To what extent this is translated into disease in the children conceived with eggs from such ovaries is a question begging for answers. This whole area clearly demands much more research.

Smoking during pregnancy

There is plenty of evidence, however, showing that smoking during pregnancy damages the unborn child.

Growing in the womb, the fetus has its own heart and blood supply but it cannot use its lungs to breathe air until after it is born. In the womb, its 'lung' is the placenta, a large mass of tissue clinging closely to the lining of the womb, where the fetal blood, pumped by the fetal heart, flows very close to the maternal blood (just as blood comes very close to the air in the lungs after birth).

The two blood supplies are separate, but substances carried in the maternal blood pass readily through the separating membranes into the fetal blood, and some waste passes out again.

The substances going to the fetus include oxygen as well as all the nutrients and building materials. Having crossed the placenta, they travel along the umbilical cord into the fetus. With them go all the undesirable components of smoke from the maternal blood. A most unwelcome pair are carbon monoxide and nicotine, both of which are found in higher concentrations in the fetus than in the mother, but there are many others besides.

Bathing baby in chemicals

The growth of a new-born baby from one egg fertilized by one sperm is a wonderfully complex chemical process, about which there is a very great deal that we don't understand. The single cell which is the fertilized egg divides again and again, and the resulting cells specialize into thousands of different kinds, all doing the right thing in the right place at the right time.

Adding in the chemicals from smoke, with their propensities for causing irritation, poisoning, mutations and cancer, doesn't seem like a good idea. There is no reason to hope that any of the constituents of tobacco smoke are kept away from the fetus and there is a wealth of evidence that specific smoke chemicals actually become more concentrated in the fetus than in the mother.

Shortage of oxygen

The carbon monoxide undoubtedly causes a shortage of oxygen for the fetus and is probably a major contributor to the failure of babies born to smoking mothers to grow as well as those who develop smoke-free. It's not just that they are smaller; they are also less robust, with a higher risk of death and disease in the early years. The lower birth weight doesn't even mean an easier delivery, because the biggest bit of the baby, the skull, is not noticeably smaller.

Restricted blood flow

The immediate effect of smoking a cigarette is to decrease the flow of blood through the placenta, and cumulative effects include damaging changes to the cells of the placenta, resulting in less blood flow. This will also contribute greatly to the failure of the fetus to grow properly. However, more subtle changes are also taking place. The hormones produced by the fetus are disturbed, though the effects these changes have on the developing child are yet to be determined. Furthermore, the accumulation of cadmium, lead and other heavy metals cannot be ignored.

Problems at birth

The observed consequences of smoking on the course of the

pregnancy, in addition to the low birth weight, are increased complications such as bleeding, early detachment of the placenta and rupture of the membranes. Many of the components of tobacco smoke could, in theory, be responsible for such effects. The risk of miscarriage is also higher, as is the risk of the baby dying at or within a few weeks of birth.

Quitting

Giving up smoking within the first three months of pregnancy allows the baby to develop to a normal birth weight. However, supported by a wealth of studies is the idea that children whose mothers smoke during their pregnancy suffer impaired development of the nervous system.

In mice, nicotine exposure before birth caused brain changes detectable after birth, while in humans, lead has been shown to cause developmental problems in the brain. By three months the brain is well advanced, so quitting at this late stage, while definitely better than carrying on smoking, is not the perfect answer.

Babies

Cot death

Cot death (or Sudden Infant Death Syndrome, SIDS) is the name given to the sudden death of infants where no other cause can be identified. They apparently just stop breathing. The highest risk is around 2–3 months of age, tailing off after about 12 months. In recent years it has been recognized that lying babies on their fronts greatly increases the risk of cot death, and a campaign to make people aware of this has been successful in halving the 1000-odd cot deaths per year in England and Wales between 1991 and 1994. Now that this cause has been virtually eliminated, smoking is the biggest remaining cause.

Here it becomes difficult to distinguish between maternal smoking during pregnancy and a smoky atmosphere for the infant to breathe, because most mothers who smoke during pregnancy continue to do so afterwards. Both seem to contribute, though another smoker sharing the house poses nearly as great a risk as a smoking mother. The risk of cot death doubles with each hour per day that the baby spends in a smoky room, and smoking probably causes nearly two-thirds of the cot deaths now in England and Wales.

Breast feeding

Breast-fed babies whose mothers smoke are also getting some smoke chemicals in their milk, which can have as much as 0.5 mg of nicotine per litre. Very roughly, the baby could be getting as much as half a cigarette's worth a day, but a 4-month-old baby is about one tenth the size of its mother, so even ignoring the extra vulnerability of children to smoking, this could be viewed as equivalent to five cigarettes a day, just in the milk. Smokers' breast milk has also been shown to contain cadmium and lead, and probably contains other toxic smoke chemicals too.

Smoking also reduces milk production by lowering the levels of prolactin, the milk-producing hormone.

Asthma

Passive smoking is quite dangerous for asthmatics. Asthma is a condition which is affecting increasing numbers of children and which, it has been suggested, could be partly due to maternal smoking during pregnancy.

However, this evidence is not yet totally convincing. Asthma is held to be the result of inhalation, probably during the first year of life, of excrement from house dust mites. These tiny creatures live off shed human skin so they are found in bedding, but dry skin debris are no use to them; the debris have to be moist and mouldy. House dust mites were virtually unknown in Victorian times but have increased rapidly since the 1920s. Their increase has paralleled the rise in asthma and has been attributed to a decline in the habit of the daily airing of beds with the bedroom windows open. Open fires, the main form of heating in Victorian times, are also great ventilators of houses. Notwithstanding this, maternal smoking could increase the susceptibility of the infant to the house dust mite.

Asthma attacks happen because the airways, sensitized in infancy, react in an exaggerated way to hostile stimuli or even to stress or anxiety. The muscles go into spasm, constricting the airways and making breathing very hard work indeed. The sufferer wheezes and struggles for breath. Extremely effective medication is available now, delivered by inhalers straight onto the surfaces of the airways, swiftly relaxing them. A smoky atmosphere increases both the frequency and severity of asthma attacks, and more medication is a poor alternative to clean air.

Children

Children living in smoky homes have cotinine levels consistent with smoking 1–2 cigarettes a week. Cotinine is a breakdown product of nicotine and is excreted in urine, where it is easily detected (likewise in saliva and blood), giving an objective measure of the degree of exposure to tobacco smoke.

Lower educational achievement

A wealth of studies have suggested lower educational achievement in the children of smokers but the reason is very hard to establish. They are certainly more likely to have time off school, and they suffer more chest infections, glue ear (the commonest cause of deafness and of hospital admission in children) and bronchitis than do children growing up in a smoke-free environment.

Cancer due to parental smoking

Children whose parents smoke during the early years of their life also run a higher risk of cancer later in their lives. On top of any risk from parents smoking before their baby is conceived, carcinogens from smoke can get through to the fetus from the mother. Umbilical cord, cord blood and placenta, all of which have to be disposed of on maternity wards, are human tissues readily available for research. Studies of umbilical cord show that, when the mother has smoked during the pregnancy, there is genetic damage in the cord of the kind that can lead to cancer. With such damage in the cord, there is no ground for hoping that it is not elsewhere in the baby. Equally, adults who smoke increase not only their own risk of many kinds of cancer but also the risk to their non-smoking spouses and their pets, so it would be surprising if children growing up in a smoky atmosphere were not in the same position.

Adults

The passive smoking argument

The argument about passive smoking raged for a long time. It is a classic example of the 'there is no evidence' type of spurious argument. As the health risks of smoking gradually seeped into public consciousness, those non-smokers who were fed up with breathing other people's smoke began to argue that the risk to their health gave them a right to clean air to breathe.

A public debate in the newspapers and broadcast media ensued, at times quite lively. The more sensitive smokers had always considered the wishes of others around them but there were plenty who, affronted at this attempt to curtail their liberty to smoke, vehemently argued that there was no evidence that passive smoking did any harm.

They were at the time reasonably right; there was very little evidence, because the search for any was not under way. There is an enormous amount of evidence now, and as a debating point the subject is all but dead, though some tobacco companies persist in reiterating the claim.

Misrepresentation

An advertising campaign in the UK national press by Philip Morris Europe SA in June 1996 tried to persuade us that the risks of passive smoking were less than those associated with, for example, eating biscuits or drinking chlorinated water. The adverts featured a table of risks, with references to the scientific publications quoted. Following complaints, they were asked by the Advertising Standards Authority to withdraw the advert on the grounds that they had misrepresented the findings of the studies quoted.

Interestingly, either no-one complained, or the ASA failed to pick up, that Philip Morris Europe SA had represented the risks of passive smoking as the risk of contracting lung cancer through passive smoking. It is a danger, but there are plenty of others too.

Lung cancer from passive smoking

Scientific opinion is that several hundred people a year die in the UK, and several thousand in the US, as a result of lung cancer contracted through passive smoking. A recent scientific paper, published in the UK, evaluated a large number of published studies on lung cancer and passive smoking from around the world. It put the risk to non-smokers of dying of lung cancer through living with a smoker as 26% higher than for living with a non-smoker.

Nevertheless, lung cancer is far from being the only hazard posed by passive smoking.

Cardiovascular disease from passive smoking

Cardiovascular disease also results from passive smoking. However, the emergence of data is echoing the history of our understanding of active smoking: some of the respiratory diseases have smoking as their main cause, so they were linked with smoking earlier than was cardiovascular disease, which has many causes. Indeed, a bad diet leads to even more cardiovascular disease than does smoking.

Heart disease risks

Nevertheless, plenty of evidence on cardiovascular disease and passive smoking is now emerging; for example, a study in Shanghai, China, found an increased risk of coronary heart disease in lifelong non-smoking Chinese women whose husbands smoked, with an even greater risk for similar women working in a smoky atmosphere. The authors concluded that urgent public health measures were needed to protect people from exposure to environmental tobacco smoke.

A paper examining passive smoking and ischaemic heart disease was published alongside the one examining the evidence on passive smoking and lung cancer. Ischaemic heart disease is due to restricted blood flow to heart muscle, and manifests itself as chest pain (angina pectoris) and heart attack (myocardial infarct). It accounts for the majority of deaths from cardiovascular disease, with strokes accounting for most of the remainder. The conclusion, based on studies from all over the world, was that non-smoking spouses of smokers were 23% more likely to die of ischaemic heart disease than were non-smokers whose spouses were also non-smokers.

Arterial thickening

These figures are backed up by a different kind of study, using ultrasound to measure the thickness of an artery wall (in the neck). The thickness of the arterial wall closely reflects hardening of the arteries, and is a reliable predictor of death from cardiovascular disease.

Smokers, ex-smokers, passive smokers and non-smokers had two sets of measurements taken, the second three years after the first. Smokers' arteries thickened 50% faster than those of non-smokers, and ex-smokers who were still passive smokers were little better off, but non-smokers exposed to as little as one hour per week of other people's smoke had 20% faster thickening. For ex-smokers now free of passive smoking, the figure was 25%.

Low exposure, high risk

Perhaps the most surprising finding in these two studies is that the risks associated with passive smoking is almost half that associated with smoking 20 cigarettes a day, despite the fact that the exposure to cigarette smoke is about 100 times greater in the smokers. This suggests that much of the risk of ischaemic heart disease occurs at a very low level of exposure to tobacco smoke. This should be borne in mind by people who assume that being a light smoker carries few risks, as well as by those who suppose that the effects of their own smoking on other people are negligible.

These important findings relate only to adults. As yet, there are no figures on arterial thickening or cardiovascular disease later in life in babies and children of smoking parents.

Nuisance value

Alongside potentially fatal diseases, the nuisance value of environmental tobacco smoke should not be forgotten. Smarting eyes, a sore throat and smelly hair and clothes are almost inevitable outcomes of sharing space with smokers. Nevertheless, for the vast majority of non-smokers, the occasional trip to a pub or smoky meeting at work will result in nothing worse. There is every reason to believe that our defences are capable of coping with the odd assault and a few minutes in a tumble drier will get the worst of the smell out of clothes.

Regular passive smoking: children

Regular exposure is another matter, even for adults, and for children it is to be strenuously avoided. The risks to children who suffer from asthma are fairly well established, as are the risks of respiratory problems. As yet to be investigated are risks to their circulatory systems. It is not appropriate to assume passive smoking is innocent until proved guilty: children should be assumed to be at risk unless proved not to be. Protecting them should extend to not smoking downstairs in the evening when there are babies or children upstairs at night – smoke rises.

Implications for families

Planning a family

For a woman smoker who intends to have children, the possibility, however remote, that she has already compromised the position of her unconceived children will not be welcome.

At this stage the possibility is little more than an idea and the risk may be extremely small. Alarm is fruitless; beyond quitting immediately, there is little which can be done. However, when planning a pregnancy there is every reason for the father to quit some months before conception.

What is beyond doubt is that maternal smoking during the pregnancy adversely affects babies in the womb, and the best course open is to heed the advice already given for so many other reasons: quit.

However, any avoidable risk is worth knowing about. For those women who don't yet smoke it should be a further incentive not to, and it should also be a discussion point for young teenage girls who are going to be on the receiving end of peer pressure and persuasive advertising.

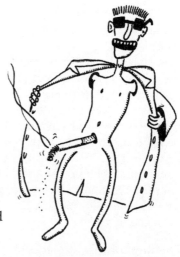

fathers should quit well before conception

Taking the matter to its logical conclusion, smokers should never smoke in the presence of females of child-bearing age or younger.

Counting the cost

Considering for a moment only the financial costs, it begins to look as though the damage done by smoking has been rather underestimated. Treating cancer can be extremely expensive. The cost to the health service of people smoking may be considerably greater than has been calculated so far.

To any parent, the thought of an ill child is distressing and to count the cost of childhood cancer only in financial terms is an insult. If one accepts that the effects of smoking may be passed on to children, either living or as yet unconceived, then smoking is of greater moral than economic importance.

Other studies on smoking in and after pregnancy point in the same direction: high quantities of genetic damage in the umbilical cord blood, smoke chemicals in breast milk, low birth weight babies, high rates of miscarriage and perinatal mortality, contribution to cot deaths: the list seems endless. That unborn and newborn children are at risk from smoking has been accepted as fact for some time. Now it seems that the unconceived child is also in danger.

The younger the person, the greater the risk

If children are at risk from parental smoking before they are even conceived, and young smokers run risks so much higher than those who start later in life, it seems reasonable to assume a sliding scale of risk from smoking, passive and active, which is high in infancy and levels off in adulthood.

Instinct has always been to protect children from smoking. This is reflected not only in law, which in many countries makes it illegal to sell tobacco products to people under a certain age, but also in the behaviour of most adults towards children where smoking is concerned. Maybe that instinct is very firmly based indeed. On scientific grounds, the age at which purchase of tobacco is allowed should be not lower than 25 . . . but on similar grounds it shouldn't be available at all.

Demographic damp squib?

We have all got used to the fact that the population is getting healthier and living longer. However, the bright, active 80 and 90 year olds of today were born back at the beginning of the century, when almost no women smoked. Most of these healthy pensioners walked or cycled to school and work. We do not yet know the state of health in old age of the children born when 40% of women and 50% of men were smokers and cars were commonplace; indeed, we don't even know about the smokers and their passive-smoker associates themselves, though prediction is easier. The 'demographic time bomb' of the population getting older may be nearing a peak.

CHAPTER 9
Old and young, quitting and smoking

Smoking and quitting

Everybody now knows that smoking causes lung cancer. Many know that it causes even more deaths from heart and circulatory disease than from cancer, and some are aware of the huge range of other diseases smokers can expect, so what makes people take up smoking?

Oscar Wilde put into words the attraction of smoking. Much-quoted, they are well worth repeating here:

> *A cigarette is the perfect type of a perfect pleasure. It is exquisite, and it leaves one unsatisfied. What more can one want?*

Given that the harm done by inhaling tobacco smoke is imperceptible to the smoker in the short term, once launched on the path of smoking there seems every reason to continue and none to stop just yet.

Smoking and age

The number of smokers has been falling in much of the developed world over the last couple of decades, indicating that the health message is beginning to get through. At the beginning of the 1970s in the UK, over 50% of men and 40% of women were smoking, but 20 years later smoking was below 30% for both groups. It sounds impressive, until you look at who is and who is not smoking.

Older and wiser

Most of the reduction is in those over 35 years of age, which at least means people are successfully quitting.

Through the decade 1982–1992, smoking was highest and steadiest amongst the 20–24-year-olds, of whom just under 40% smoked, with a reduction of only 2% in the number of smokers over the decade.

During the same period, smoking among 35–49-year-olds dropped by 20% while the 50–59-year-olds reduced their smoking by 27% and the over-60s by 35%. It is in the middle years of life that smokers become increasingly aware of the effects of smoking on their own health, providing belated motivation to quit. Furthermore, one smoker in two dies prematurely as a result of smoking, so the older age groups lose smokers this way, too.

Young and immortal

However, the rate of smoking in youngsters aged 11–15 is not going down. Smoking is effectively gaining its new recruits from the young, whose sense of immortality obliterates any belief in the health risks and who are particularly susceptible to advertising and to the attitudes of their friends. Moreover, they are recruited at an age when their health is particularly vulnerable; someone starting at the age of 15 is four to five times as likely to die of lung cancer as someone starting after the age of 25, and there is no reason to suppose that the situation with cardiovascular disease is any different.

At the age of 15, the percentage regularly smoking (at least one cigarette a week, but averaging more than 50 per week for this age group) is approaching the overall adult rate and is well over half the peak adult rate. However, there is one important difference in many developed countries: the percentage of girls smoking is higher than the percentage of boys. There are two implications here: firstly, a large proportion of smokers are recruited before the age of 16, i.e. before it is even legal for them to buy cigarettes, and secondly, the rate of smoking among women is set to overtake the rate in men.

Figures for Britain in 1994 show that 28% of 15-year-olds were regular smokers. In the same year, 28% of all adult men and 26% of all adult women smoked, with the figures for the age group when smoking peaks, 20–24, being 40% for men and 38% for women. These figures come from OPCS surveys; other sources give slightly different figures, but they all agree on the trends.

Who smokes?

A classless society?

As far as smoking goes, we are a long way from a classless society. Smoking rates (1992) were highest for unskilled and manual workers (42% of men and 35% of women) and lowest for professionals (14% of men and 13% of women). The same profile was true 20 years earlier, though with considerably higher rates, i.e. professional men and women 33% and unskilled manual workers 64% of men and 42% of women. Not only are fewer professionals smoking, the rate of decline in their smoking has been steeper.

Influences on children

The younger smokers start, the more likely they are to have done it out of a desire to have the 'right' image, resentment about being told what to do (i.e. 'don't smoke'), and a feeling that worrying about serious things is something for adults, not them. They are also likely to take up smoking casually, because a friend offers them a cigarette, and to enjoy the challenge of keeping it secret from their parents and obtaining the cigarettes despite being under-age. Few set out with the intention of becoming addicted; indeed, most feel that they won't, but the fact is that by the second or third cigarette, it's probably too late.

Children are far more likely to smoke if their brothers, sisters or parents smoke, and girls more so than boys. Whether their friends smoke is also a factor: anecdotally, almost all smokers cite 'being in with the crowd' or some such as a reason for starting. In England in 1994, 26% of boys and 30% of girls were regular smokers at the age of 15, and roughly half as many were occasional smokers. Fewer than a third had never tried smoking. Money seems to be a limiting factor; children who smoke have more disposable money than those who don't and, despite the law, very few seem to have significant trouble buying cigarettes.

Advertising

However, there is another important factor in influencing whether individual children smoke: their exposure to advertising. Youngsters almost all declare that they are not affected by advertising; however, this is not what the advertising agencies believe nor, according to the tobacco company documents now being made public in North America, is it what the tobacco companies believe.

"We don't smoke that s---"
The following extract really says it all:

> Dave Goerlitz, R J Reynold's lead model for seven years, ...
> portrayed the rugged smoker who could scale mountains with one
> hand while casually dragging on a cigarette in Winston
> advertisements. Goerlitz appeared in 42 ads throughout the
> 1980s, smoking three packs a day throughout the rigorous
> sessions. He says his marketing brief was to "attract young
> smokers to replace the older ones who were dying or quitting".
>
> During one shoot on top of Mount Evans in Colorado, Goerlitz,
> gasping for breath, suddenly realized he was the only smoker on
> the mountain. Turning to an R J Reynolds executive accom-
> panying him, Goerlitz politely inquired why he did not smoke.
>
> "I will never forget what he said. The executive said 'We don't
> smoke that s---; we just sell it. We just reserve the right to smoke
> for the young, the poor, the black and the stupid.'"
>
> At the time, Goerlitz simply laughed. "I was arrogant. I was part
> of the scam, selling an image to young boys. My job was to get
> half a million kids smoking by 1995."
>
> *(Reproduced with permission from Come to Cancer Country: Who's Lucky Now?,*
> *by Janine di Giovanni, The Sunday Times, 2.8.92.)*

David Goerlitz subsequently suffered a stroke, but it was visiting
his brother in a cancer clinic, and being asked to leave because he was
recognized as the Winston man, which changed him into a vehement
anti-smoking campaigner.

Reg
A highly successful campaign ('Reg') was run in Scotland, the north
of England and parts of Wales, by Imperial Tobacco, until they were
forced by the Advertising Standards Authority to withdraw it because
it appealed more to children than to adults. The Health Education
Authority had lodged the complaint and were subsequently involved
in a study of the campaign and its effect on children.

Reg was a smoker who made weak jokes and flippant remarks,
which the 14–15-year-olds, in particular, found entertaining. The
campaign played successfully upon the rebellious feelings of this age
group and, according to several youngsters interviewed about it,
effectively 'gave them permission to smoke'. It is a sad irony that the

permission was welcome and that in not doing as they were told by authority figures in their lives, they did as they were told by the tobacco company – but then, advertisers spend serious money on making their message so subtle that it persuades people to do something they wouldn't otherwise do.

Teenagers smoke the most advertised brands

A number of studies have shown that advertising appeals to, and influences, children far more than adults. A large US study showed that the three most advertised brands of cigarettes had 35% of the total market between them but 86% of the teenage market. The teenagers switched brands to follow the adverts.

The weight question

Cigarette advertising is also targeted at young women, emphasizing women's brands, with names like 'slim'. Given the increase in women smoking, the message about cigarettes making them slim, lovely, youthful and glamorous has presumably bitten deep. Funny that the ads missed out the wrinkles, yellowing skin and teeth, thickening waist, smell and disease . . .

. . . but in any case, the weight question is somewhat misrepresented. Many scientific observations support the idea that smokers tend to have a lower body mass index, i.e. weigh less for their height. However, this is only part of the story.

Pot bellies?

What the cigarette adverts don't say is that smoking changes body shape, increasing the waist-to-hip ratio. Exaggerating slightly to illustrate the point, despite weighing less, smokers tend to be pot-bellied with spindly legs. This is probably due to smoking upsetting the levels of hormones; irrespective of smoking, such a body fat distribution is associated with high blood pressure, heart disease

Pot-bellied with spindly legs

89

and diabetes. Another curiosity is that, although the waist-to-hip ratio increases with the amount smoked, the body mass index does not go on decreasing. This may be because heavy smokers are simply more unfit and so less prone to exercise.

Getting hooked

'Getting hooked' is a neat term for a complex process, part of which is minute structural changes in the brain.

Nicotine is not a naturally occurring substance in the body, but there are sites sensitive to chemical messengers in the brain and throughout the body with which nicotine can interfere. Not only does it affect the signaling going on, its continued presence quickly modifies some of the signaling equipment. The most obvious manifestation of this is that most smokers felt sick with their first and possibly second cigarette but not with subsequent ones. Other examples which are less apparent are the addictive changes.

One of the nicotine-induced changes which takes place in the brain when someone takes up smoking illustrates the process of addiction, in a simplified manner. The nicotine occupies sites which would normally be used by the brain's own messengers, so the brain cells actually grow extra sites. When the smoker tries to quit, there are all the extra nicotine-sensitive sites with nothing to satisfy their hunger, so craving and withdrawal set in. The sites have to be dismantled before the craving stops and this can take much longer than getting hooked. About 90% of those who get as far as their fourth cigarette are hooked and end up as long-term smokers, but quitting can take months.

Maintaining nicotine levels

Every regular smoker smokes to achieve (first thing in the morning), and then maintain, a particular level of nicotine in the blood. The level varies from smoker to smoker but in any individual it is remarkably constant from day to day.

The nicotine yield from a cigarette varies with the way it is smoked, and smokers given a supplement of nicotine actually modify their smoking, taking fewer or shorter drags or stubbing out sooner, so they end up with the same level of nicotine as they would have had just smoking cigarettes. Smokers given a cigarette higher in nicotine than their usual brand can even find it 'too strong' and 'unpleasant'.

Genetic influence

Most of the nicotine which gets into the body is broken down to cotinine by an enzyme (known as CYP2A6). Some people produce ineffective versions of this enzyme and so break down their nicotine more slowly. Research has shown that such people are less likely to become smokers even though they have experimented with smoking. Furthermore, those who do become smokers smoke fewer cigarettes. This has clear implications for understanding the addictiveness of cigarettes and even suggests that interfering with this enzyme may offer a way of preventing smoking and helping smokers quit.

Sheer pleasure

There is far more to getting hooked, though: not only changes in the brain but the social and behavioural aspects of smoking, which can be very positive. Some people smoke to have the right image or to be 'one of the crowd', some use cigarettes to bridge awkward social situations. Some find it relieves stress, calms them when angry or cheers them up. Smoking soon becomes part of normal behaviour and there is a habit as well as an addiction to be broken.

Finally, not least among the factors in getting hooked is the sheer pleasure to be had from smoking. Oscar Wilde knew all about it.

Quitting

For anyone hooked, quitting is not an easy thing to do and despite the wish of most smokers that they were non-smokers, at best only one serious, planned and supported attempt in ten actually succeeds. About 2 million people attempt to quit on the UK's annual No Smoking Day but three months later only 30 000 (1.5%) are still not smoking.

Older people are the great quitters. According to some of the ex-smokers quoted in Chapter 11, an important crunch point was the conviction that their own health was suffering. For others, appreciation of the likely risks or the social unacceptability is enough, but for all smokers, quitting is difficult.

Aids to quitting

Several aids to quitting and places to seek more detailed help are suggested below but none of them will do the quitting themselves. At best they will make it marginally easier, but this could still be the difference between success and failure so they are worth considering.

Preparing for quitting gives the greatest possible chance of success. For instance, it is useful for anyone contemplating quitting to work out why and where they smoke and plan to either avoid the situations or have an alternative, for example something to suck or fiddle with instead of a cigarette.

Exercise

Lots of people find exercise helpful in overcoming the craving for a smoke and there are good reasons why this works. Whatever is uppermost in the mind has just won the constant battle for attention; signals coming into the brain have to be filtered and selected so that the important ones are dealt with and the others ignored. If you are sitting down, you are not, till you read this, aware of the pressure of your bottom on the seat, although the information is being constantly sent to the brain.

When consciousness is filled with the desire to smoke, exercise will vastly increase the range of new information coming in and the brain will have to compare its urgency with the need for a cigarette. Already the strength of the 'smoke' signal has been diluted and, if the activity is absorbing enough, the signal will be switched off altogether.

This is true for any absorbing occupation, but exercise alters the whole activity state of the body. Blood flow increases, sluggish areas get flushed out and subtle hormonal responses to the exercise increase the sense of well-being. In addition, exercise actively counters some of the damage resulting from smoking and should reinforce the decision to quit.

Many people are encouraged to smoke and discouraged from quitting by the notion that smoking keeps their weight down. Some people even think of taking up smoking to get their weight down, but there are far better ways. Although about 20% of smokers actually lose weight on quitting, and the average weight gain, 0.5–1 kg, is smaller than most people suppose, it is as well to plan to thwart any weight gain on quitting. Improving the diet and increasing the exercise will make it easier to quit, address the weight question and improve the complexion and sense of well-being. The saving on tobacco will easily fund the fresh fruit and vegetables, and the exercise can be free.

Glucose

Another trick worth trying (except for diabetics) is crunching a glucose tablet. These are sold on sweet counters and in chemist's shops as an energy boost for sportspeople. A preliminary study has found that, when compared with artificial sweeteners, they reduced the craving for a cigarette and also increased the smoking abstinence rates over a 4-week period. More extensive studies are planned. The action of a sudden rise in blood glucose, which is absorbed within a few minutes when eaten, is to release insulin. Via the release of messenger chemicals in the brain, insulin influences the part of the brain controlling appetite, be it for food or cigarettes. It might also help to keep down the excess consumption of food which leads to weight gain. A whole pack of glucose tablets has the same calorific value as a slice of bread but, taken one at a time, many times the satiety value.

Cutting or glutting?

A good launch for a successful bid to quit could be a deliberate surfeit. Several people who have quit reported doing so after a day of heavy smoking, when they suddenly found the habit disgusting and just stopped.

Conversely, cutting down as opposed to stopping totally has a very poor rate of success indeed. Smokers tend to control the delivery of nicotine by altering the depth and rate of drags, getting more nicotine from each cigarette when they cut down on the number they smoke. Moreover, when they do cut down sufficiently to lower their blood nicotine levels, the craving gets worse and worse. There is ample evidence to show that smoking is controlled to keep the level of nicotine in the blood not only high enough to avoid withdrawal but also below that at which it becomes unpleasant, so a little deliberate extra smoking should easily result in a useful degree of disgust.

Nicotine replacement

One way to boost the chances is with nicotine patches or chewing gum, which are available over the counter from chemists. They work by supplying a background level of nicotine, which damps down the craving, but they do not replicate the nicotine levels achieved by smoking. For one thing, the nicotine level rises much more slowly, and for another, it doesn't get so high.

A new product on the market supplies nicotine via a small plastic tube which is sucked on, very much like a cigarette. Nicotine is delivered mainly to the mouth and throat, from where it is absorbed. An alternative provides inhalable nicotine in an nasal spray, which makes the nicotine delivery more like smoking, though users can find it somewhat irritant in the nose.

Nicotine supplements are not available on NHS prescription so have to be bought at the commercial rate, though a private prescription (available from GPs) will save the VAT. Anyone contemplating using nicotine supplements should find out about them before deciding. Any pharmacy should have information leaflets and the pharmacist will be prepared to advise as to what they can do and which sort to use. If, for example, part of the appeal of smoking is something in the mouth, then the inhaler or chewing gum could well be better than the patches. Conversely, for anyone wanting to give up without advertising the fact to the world at large, the patches might be best.

Having decided to use nicotine replacement, establishing the correct quantity of nicotine for the individual and their smoking habit is important. Too little may be ineffective and too much can be, at the very least, unpleasant; either could undermine the attempt to quit. A reputable pharmacy will not sell it without first discussing the user's particular needs, and the pharmacist will always be pleased to help. Quitters may also wish to get advice from a doctor and take advantage of any help and support she or he can offer.

However, without determination to stop, nicotine alone stands a very small chance of working. No-one should expect it to do the quitting for them, only to put quitting within their grasp.

Where to get help

Detailed advice on quitting is available from many places. Most GP's surgeries have leaflets and many run smoking cessation clinics or will help on an individual basis. Dispensing chemists also have leaflets and the pharmacist can offer advice. In addition, there are telephone helplines advertised in the aforementioned leaflets.

Quit, a charity devoted to helping people off tobacco, offers a range of advice both over their free helpline 0800 00 22 00 and as printed matter. They will talk and listen to anyone, they don't lecture but they do have practical advice to offer and a 'break free' information pack which they will send to youngsters, though they insist they won't send it out to parents who want to pass it on to their children! Their 'break free' pack is just one of a range of information packs, designed for all kinds of people.

For those whose morale is boosted by reading about anything

from the iniquities of the global tobacco industry to the very latest in health information, ASH (Action on Smoking and Health) would be worth contacting. They will send out their catalogue to anyone sending an A5-sized stamped addressed envelope. They keep a wealth of up-to-date and inexpensive reading matter on all aspects of smoking and the tobacco industry, a small proportion of which is free.

Names, addresses and telephone numbers are at the beginning of this book.

Not starting

Current statistics on youngsters and smoking may surprise people unfamiliar with teenagers. By the age of 15, roughly two thirds have experimented with smoking and nearly one third are regular smokers. The number who have experimented with smoking is greater than the highest prevalence of smoking (around 40% in the 20–24-year-old age group), which means that by the age of 15 at least some have tried and rejected it. Who are they and how did they do it?

Out in the open

Those least likely to become regular smokers are those whose home environment is one in which smoking is discussed openly and honestly, and this is an even stronger influence than whether there are smokers in the family. Clearly, it is possible for parents who smoke to persuade their children that it is better not to start. Forewarned is forearmed: discussing the health effects of smoking, the difference between the image presented by adverts and the reality of smoking, and thinking in advance about what to do when offered a cigarette is excellent protection for a child, and it can hardly start too early. Very young children are aware of smoking and of adverts (some 6-year-olds can spot cigarette brand names on Formula 1 racing cars) and to leave them alone with the ideas put over by tobacco advertising is hardly fair to them.

Girls are now more likely than boys to smoke, and one presumption, borne out by recent surveys, is that they perceive smoking as an adjunct to that most urgent of current concerns, staying slim. Such perceptions are strengthened by advertising, but apart from the fact that the average effect of smoking in reducing weight is small, and that smoking can even cause weight gain in a few, the object of being slim is to be attractive. The fact that smoking attacks the skin, thickens the waist and fouls the breath needs pointing out. There are far better ways of staying slim and, as mentioned before, a good diet with plenty of exercise has the added advantage of improving health and enhancing the complexion. It is also a great deal less expensive.

What are cigarette ads really trying to tell us?

Campaigns

Over the years from 1984 to 1994, children's awareness of the health risks increased but there was almost no decrease in the numbers smoking. It seems that though 99% of them know that smoking causes lung cancer, they somehow don't see it applying to them.

School-based anti-smoking campaigns in various countries other than the UK are successful in turning some young smokers into ex-smokers and in delaying the start of smoking in others. They are a valuable tool in prevention of smoking-related disease.

Children who smoke are more aware of, and knowledgeable about, cigarette adverts. Such awareness in non-smoking children is a good predictor of whether they are going to start smoking in the next year. Tobacco companies are shy about admitting how much they spend on advertising but it is something like ten times what the Government spends on anti-smoking health promotion.

There is overwhelming evidence from around the world that banning tobacco advertising leads to a drop in the number of smokers of all ages, but particularly children. This drop in smoking is, in some countries, with the advertising provided by sports sponsorship still intact, and even those countries which have banned tobacco company sponsorship of domestic sports are stuck, at least for the next few years, with its most famous image, Formula 1 racing, which takes place around the world.

A more subtle development in brand promotion involves cross-marketing, i.e. selling clothes or other merchandise under the cigarette brand name. Tenuous as this may seem as a cigarette advertising technique, it works.

As and when the promotion of smoking, including cross-marketing and sports sponsorship (soon to be banned, at least in developed countries), is totally eradicated, and cigarettes come in standardized packs designed to rob them of their advertising value (not yet planned in the UK, though under consideration in Canada), children will only have adult example and peer pressure to contend with – and current peer pressure is moulded by cigarette advertising.

Blood pressure as a predictor?

There is one factor predictive of smoking behaviour which has nothing whatsoever to do with the tobacco companies: blood pressure. As part of the British Birth Cohort Study, a study over many years of 5000 children, all born in the same week, showed that a low blood pressure and slow pulse rate at the age of 10 was a surprisingly good predictor of the child being a smoker by the age of 16. Some doctors recognize a personality type (artistic, introspective, easily tired and depressed) as associated with low blood pressure. There has long been recognized a surprising anomaly with smoking: despite the arterial damage caused by smoking, which ought to result in raised blood pressure, smokers as a group don't have particularly high blood pressure. One explanation could be that smokers, as a group, start with lower blood pressure than the average population.

If those most likely to become dependent on smoking start out with a low pulse rate and blood pressure, then screening and making them aware of the situation is a possibility. No-one gets addicted to cigarettes without first trying one and at least those most at risk could be warned that they are likely to end up heavily addicted to smoking unless they guard against starting. That they would have more difficulty stopping than others seems likely but it is far from proven; this seems like yet another case where more research is needed. Care would also need be taken not to give false confidence to those whose blood pressure and heart rate are not low.

Getting the message through

At the September 1998 meeting of the British Association for the Advancement of Science, Professor Richard Peto of the Nuffield Department of Clinical Medicine, Oxford, delivered some good news. In the past 25 years, the number of middle-aged (35–69 years) British men and women killed every year by smoking has halved, from 80 000 to 40 000. This is the largest decline in the world, and demonstrates clearly that the health message is getting through and persuading people to quit. Despite this, smoking remains by far the biggest avoidable killer – but 25 years ago it was even worse.

Such a reduction in middle-age deaths is impressive, but there is huge cause for concern in the rising number of under-age smokers, to whom the health message seemingly means little. Children must now be at the centre of efforts to reduce the toll of disease and death from smoking.

Links between blood pressure and tendency to smoke may turn out to be important, though at this stage the findings are preliminary. Attacking tobacco promotion has been shown in several countries to be effective, so is definitely important. Discussing smoking fully, honestly and frequently with children, at home as well as in school, and promoting amongst people of all ages a better understanding of the health issues, are arguably the most important of all.

CHAPTER 10
Rescue therapy

Is there anything a smoker can do, short of cutting down or giving up, to lessen the health risks?

The answer is probably – cautiously – yes.

Diet, both what to eat and what to avoid, and exercise, are important in redressing some of the damage done by smoking.

Diet: what to eat

The overall risk of cardiovascular disease can certainly be minimized by following the kind of diet recommended to almost anyone, including athletes, by almost everyone these days: plenty of fresh fruit and vegetables, not too much fat, with the fat tending towards vegetable and fish sources and away from animal fats. The same diet is also recommended for lessening the risk of cancer.

There is a lot of attention at present given to vitamins A, C and E, the so-called 'anti-oxidant' vitamins. Oxidants play a role in emphysema and cardiovascular disease, but they are also thought to increase the risk of many other diseases, including cancers. The levels of vitamins A and C, though not E, in the plasma of male Scottish smokers have been shown to be lower than in non-smokers, though quite why, or what this means, remains to be established. Oxidation is promoted by many of the agents in smoke, so a few vitamins to protect against it sounds like a good idea – rather like a bit of long-term polish on the silver and brass. In addition, some of the B-group vitamins (notably folic acid but also B6 and B12) can lower levels of homocysteine in blood, thus reducing the risk of cardiovascular disease.

Pills or food?

What is not so clear is whether popping a vitamin pill once a day is the answer. A study was done on AIDS sufferers, looking into vitamin A as a means of alleviating some of their problems. AIDS patients took extra vitamin A, either as carrots or as pills. It was arguable how large the beneficial effect of the carrots was, but those on the tablets appeared to do worse than those without any extra vitamin A.

Another intriguing story is the role of calcium in kidney stones, which are made of calcium oxalate. Taking calcium supplements in tablet form, including indigestion tablets, increases the risk of kidney stones, although a diet high in calcium-rich foods seems to reduce the risk.

We don't know everything about what is in food. 'Potatoes contain lots of water, potatoes satisfy hunger, therefore water satisfies hunger' is clearly a nonsense. Essential compounds of whose nutritional value we have so far been unaware are still being 'discovered'. Indeed, research into such compounds is currently very fashionable, and doubtless in the future we will be astounded at our ignorance right now.

The overall message is that some of the damage done by smoking may be counteracted by increasing the intake of various vitamins, but that to do so by taking the vitamins in the form of pills may well be less effective than eating foods which are rich in the vitamins.

Vitamin A

Vitamins are not without their dangers, as some polar explorers found to their cost. Back at the beginning of the 20th century, before a radio call could bring in rescue or life-saving supplies, men (there were no women polar explorers in those days) were occasionally driven to such extremes that they killed and ate, sometimes raw, any creatures they could catch. In their debilitated state, most of the meat was too tough to chew but the liver was an exception. The discovery and understanding of vitamins was in its infancy during this period and the explorers had no idea that dangerously (to humans) large concentrations of vitamin A are stored in the liver of some animals.

Units for measuring vitamin A

The most often-quoted example is the polar bear, whose liver can contain 12 000 retinol equivalents per gram – and here we need an aside. Vitamin A is not a unique substance but is any of a number of substances possessing the same biological activity as retinol. For this reason, when considering their activity as 'vitamin A', they are usually measured not by weight (usually mg or μg: 1 milligram = one thousandth of a gram and 1 microgram = one millionth of a gram) but in 'retinol equivalents'. Six μg of β-carotene, the kind of vitamin A found in carrots, is one retinol equivalent, i.e. it has the same effect as 1 μg of retinol.

Don't eat polar bear liver

The maximum daily recommended intake of vitamin A ranges from 400 retinol equivalents for a child to 1000 for an adult male and 1200 for a mother who is breast feeding, so half a pound of raw polar bear liver could contain enough vitamin A for six years' breast feeding or eighteen years of childhood.

The immediate symptoms of sudden (acute) overdose, which would be a single dose of 500 000 retinol equivalents (a mouthful or so of polar bear liver) or 50 000 retinol equivalents per day over a week or so, are drowsiness, sluggishness, an irresistible desire to sleep, headache, irritability, nausea and, after 24 hours, peeling of the skin.

Sir Douglas Mawson

Sir Douglas Mawson, one the greatest of Antarctic explorers, who mapped 2000 miles of Antarctic coast and contributed enormously to the scientific knowledge of the region, is believed to have suffered from vitamin A overdose through eating husky dog livers.

On the second of his three Antarctic expeditions, the Australasian Antarctic Expedition, 1911–1914, he and a companion on a sledging trip were left with little food and equipment when the third member of their party perished down a deep crevasse with sledge, stores and dogs. They were 300 miles from their base and their only hope was to eat the remaining six dogs, for whom there was now no food, as they travelled. Three and a half weeks later and 100 miles from base, his companion died, having lost the skin from his legs and developed digestive disorders and delirium.

Mawson, his legs, fingers, lips and nose also raw, carried on alone. A few days later the soles of his feet blistered off. Eight weeks after the original accident he regained the base, helped by a cache of food reached ten days previously. Only years later were the skin and digestive problems diagnosed as due to excessive vitamin A from the dog livers.

Vitamin A and pregnancy: moderation

On a more immediately relevant note, pregnant women are now advised to avoid excess vitamin A, as huge quantities can cause birth defects in their babies. This doesn't mean cutting out carrots, but it does mean avoiding liver and not stuffing down multi-vitamin pills.

Seeing in the dark

Total avoidance of vitamin A is not a good idea because it is essential for, among other things, good vision, especially night vision. It is used by the inner light-sensitive surface of the eye, the retina, to changing light into nerve signals: hence the name 'retinol'.

Night blindness, a result of too little vitamin A in the diet, was described by the Egyptians around 1500 BC. Though they didn't link it to dietary deficiency, they treated it with topical application of fried or roasted liver. Maybe enough seeped through the skin to make a difference, or perhaps licking the fingers clean after placing it over the face was enough. Very probably sufficient was left over after treatment to make a meal.

Vitamins: fat or water soluble

An important aspect of vitamin A is that it is fat-soluble (as are vitamins K and E). The other vitamins are all water-soluble.

With water-soluble vitamins, eating more than is needed leads to excretion of the excess in urine. This makes overdose unlikely, though the flip side is that we do have to maintain a reasonably steady intake of them to avoid deficiency. The fat-soluble vitamins are the reverse: they can be easily stored in the body but are hard to get rid of when an excess has been eaten. During the second world war some studies were done on vitamin depletion in the diet. Lack of vitamin C soon manifested itself but 200 days elapsed before those avoiding vitamin A began to show any ill effects. We seem to be able to store up enough carotene while carrots are in season to last all year. Nevertheless, smokers seem to have low levels of carotenes, so may benefit from slightly more in their diets.

Fresh fruit and veg

Vitamin C

Vitamin C must be the best-known of the vitamins. Nearly all fruits, especially citrus fruits and strawberries, fresh vegetables and even potatoes are useful sources of vitamin C.

In the experiments in which smoke-laden plasma flowing over healthy blood vessel endothelium led to inflammatory phagocytes and platelets sticking to the walls, pre-loading the plasma with vitamin C at a level easily achieved in humans by dietary means lessened the effect. If this translates into an overall action of vitamin C in preventing damage to vessel endothelium by smoke chemicals then sucking oranges or eating any vitamin C-rich fruit or vegetable is definitely a good idea. Furthermore, it has been found that smokers have reduced plasma levels of vitamin C, suggesting that a little extra in the diet might be useful.

Vitamin E

The same researchers who tried vitamin C as protection for blood vessel endothelium against smoke-laden plasma also tried vitamin E on the grounds that it, too, is an anti-oxidant. It did not have the same preventive effect as vitamin C: a potent example of how complex all these interactions are.

Vitamin E was first isolated in 1936 from wheatgerm oil, the germ being the bit of the grain of wheat from which the new plant will begin to sprout. Its existence was deduced 14 years earlier when it was found that rats could not sustain a pregnancy without some component of the oil.

Vitamin E in the lungs of smokers

There is currently some interest in vitamin E in the lungs of smokers, where there is considerably less than in non-smokers. So far, there is no direct information about the role of vitamin E in human lungs, but the ability of inflammatory phagocytes from smokers' lungs to destroy rat lung cells was reduced when the lung cells had plenty of vitamin E.

It has also been shown that lung cancer patients and their families have reduced levels of both vitamin E and selenium (see below) in their lungs, though so far there is no indication as to whether this is due to dietary factors, a response to smoking or passive smoking, or a genetically based difference.

Giving vitamin E supplements to smokers raised the quantity in their lungs, but not to the levels found in non-smokers. There is no demonstration yet that extra vitamin E could protect smokers' lungs, but it is an anti-oxidant and emphysema is caused, at least partly, by oxidation, so a diet rich in vitamin E seems like a good bet. Useful sources include eggs, green leafy vegetables, and corn and peanut oils. In addition, there is reputed to be no toxicity associated with excess vitamin E, unlike vitamin A.

Vitamin E in the body

In humans, vitamin E seems to act on structures deep within the cell, which implies a very broad range of functional effects.

In many animals, and probably also in man, vitamin E somehow protects the walls of the red blood cells from breaking down. It also could be important in keeping muscles healthy, including the heart muscle, but the medical literature is sprinkled with failures to demonstrate clearly that vitamin E treatment actually improves matters.

However, requirements for it rise when the diet is high in polyunsaturated fats because it prevents toxic oxidation products being formed. Polyunsaturated fats are the ones we are all encouraged to eat now for the sake of our arteries, in preference to the saturated animal fats.

Selenium

In man, the element selenium seems to overlap with vitamin E in its actions, so that a dietary deficiency of vitamin E alone can be made up for. Selenium is commonly found with vitamins A, C and E in the 'anti-oxidant' dietary supplements currently on sale.

Other dietary alternatives to vitamin E, such as the coenzyme Q series, have also been identified. Nature often produces more than one solution to a problem and it is no surprise that several different compounds are capable of job-sharing in our bodies.

Selenium has an interesting history: back in the early days of semiconductors, when people were experimenting with doping slices of high-purity silicon or germanium with various elements to make diodes and transistors, selenium and tellurium were found to work well, but at a price. The people involved developed severe bad breath which took months to subside – an overpowering indication that selenium does something in the lungs. They had absorbed the elements through their skin.

Selenium is absorbed from the soil by crops such as wheat. In farmland poor in selenium, it can be added as part of the fertilizer mix applied.

Vitamins B6, B12 and folic acid

All three of these can lower the levels of homocysteine in blood. Folic acid is currently advised for all women planning pregnancy, as lack of it can cause serious birth defects. It is found in green leafy vegetables, liver and yeast, and so important is it deemed to be in avoiding cardiovascular disease that some people are even contemplating adding it to flour, which almost everyone eats, to raise dietary intake. As smokers are at risk of cardiovascular damage and disease, extra folic acid could possibly provide some protection.

Vitamin B6, too, is found in yeast and liver, as well as in lean meat, milk, grains and egg yolk. B12 comes from liver, kidney, lean meat, fish and eggs. With yeast a source of folic acid and B6, one is tempted to wonder whether beer might be as good for the heart as red wine.

Diet: what to avoid

So much for the foods to eat – what of the ones to avoid? The rationale here is not so much to counteract the effects of smoke as to minimize damage which would add to that done by smoking.

Fat is the culprit, but there are many kinds of fat and some are more of a problem than others. Here is where it all goes a bit hazy in the supermarket. Strict regulations forbid manufacturers to claim that their brand of cooking oil is positively good for blood vessels and a natural reticence will prevent them from labeling their biscuits as 'high in the most artery-clogging kind of fat known to mankind'. What shoppers seem to need to know are the code words: saturated, polyunsaturated, monounsaturated, triglycerides, low density lipoproteins, highly confusing gobbledygook . . . forget it. To quote a recent Chief Medical Officer, 'of course you can have butter on your toast – just don't have too much'.

The other thing to bear in mind is that when our forebears lived a far more physically active life, bacon was prized for its fat not its lean. It's a fair bet that animal fat is a greater danger to the car-driving deskbound worker of today than it was to the walking labourer of our grandparents' day.

The overall message on diet and smoking is to eat the kind of diet recommended for a healthy heart: plenty of fresh fruit and vegetables but only moderate quantities of fat, which should include more from fish and vegetable sources than from animal sources. Bread, pasta, rice and other cereal-based foods are fine, but watch out for too much butter on the toast. Cakes, biscuits, crisps etc. are all there to be enjoyed but are better not forming a regular part of the diet; they will do nothing to counteract the effects of smoking. Red wine is positively beneficial up to the point where inebriation brings its own risk of disaster, or the alcohol begins to rot the liver.

An improvement in diet can have an impact on some of the damage done by smoking, but the best diet on earth is not a substitute for quitting.

Exercise

Exercise is at least as important as diet in helping to counteract some of the damage done by smoking. Again, moderation is probably better than vast helpings. Gentle steady exercise such as walking or cycling will do a lot to help the circulation. The full effects of exercise on the cardiovascular system are complex. Even quite gentle activities

give rise to a cascade of subtle but beneficial changes, some of which involve the chemical messengers in the endothelial cells lining the vessel walls. Included in the effects are less prickly platelets and calmer inflammatory phagocytes, better regulation of clotting and lower blood pressure due to better condition of artery walls.

Athletes at rest have low blood pressure and pulse rates, which means that they are being very efficient at pumping the blood around their bodies. High blood pressure means that the heart is straining to force the blood round against massive resistance and, aside from those whose blood pressure is high because their control systems are doing the wrong things, the high resistance is due to the narrowing, stiffening and blockage or partial blockage of arteries.

Get the blood moving

The secret to effective gentle exercise is to get the blood flowing along nicely for long enough to flush out the complete system.

When blood slows down or even stands still, as it can particularly in the leg veins of someone inactive for long periods, or even in the arteries where eddies form around branch points or atheroma, the platelets sink out of what little stream is left and settle on the vessel endothelium. Older platelets are fairly stable but younger ones (the lifespan of a platelet in human blood is about 10 days) can be a bit jumpy and flip over into clot-forming mode, releasing chemical signals which trigger other platelets into doing the same. Before you know it, fibrin strings are forming, a clot is under way and the inflammatory phagocytes gather.

In smokers, there is additional danger from 1), inflammatory phagocytes which, being angry, can start chewing at the vessel walls; 2), smoke-excited platelets and 3), direct damage to the endothelial cells by the smoke chemicals. This damage in itself attracts the platelets in to form a clot.

If the blood is flowing smoothly past, far fewer platelets and inflammatory phagocytes will even touch the walls, let alone settle on them, and any spilled messenger chemicals will be swept away and diluted in the blood at large. They will eventually be mopped up and recycled.

The same holds good for smoke chemicals. Given that they are in the blood, the best thing is to keep them moving until they can be broken down (mainly in the liver) or offloaded (mainly via the kidneys).

How much exercise?

To achieve this kind of blood flow doesn't take 300 sit-ups, a five-mile run or a work-out at the gym. All it needs is a quiet walk, keeping up a steady rhythm for as little as 20–30 minutes. The effect is to gently raise the rate at which the blood is moving, washing away any local build-ups of clotting factors or angry inflammatory phagocytes and bathing the area in ordinary unexcited blood whose phagocytes are more disposed to do a few quiet repairs than to rise up and chew the walls, and whose platelets aren't over-eager to form clots.

There is another benefit to a walk. Assuming the walk doesn't include indulgence in a cigarette, the increased depth and rate of breathing will shift extra clean air in and out of the lungs, helping to clear out a little of the smoke residue that is building up and also allowing the inflammatory phagocytes time to calm down. The increased blood flow through the lungs will promote such repair as is possible to the lung tissue digested by the angry inflammatory phagocytes.

It doesn't have to be a walk. Cycling, dancing, mowing the lawn, sweeping, vacuuming, or a few lengths of the swimming pool will do as well and add variety. The important thing is that it should be fairly steady, should last a reasonable length of time and should be done regularly, like about five times a week.

Guaranteed

Guarantees are rare but this kind of exercise comes with one firmly attached. If this is more than the normal quantity of activity, anyone in a reasonably ordinary state of health will notice an improved sense of well-being surprisingly soon.

Deskbound?

Anyone who is deskbound can do a fair bit for their leg veins by taking a few deep breaths from time to time. The negative pressure created inside the chest cavity by the breathing muscles (diaphragm, rib muscles) in order to suck in air will also suck up blood from the abdominal and leg veins. Wiggling the toes, rotating the ankles, tapping the feet, drumming the heels and generally fidgeting will do a lot to stop 'pooling' of blood in the veins, something which can, if other circumstances are unfavourable, lead to varicose veins or to clotting.

The mechanisms by which exercise can help counteract some of the damage done by smoking have only been skated over here. Other more subtle and complex changes take place, too, all of them to the benefit of the exerciser. Exercise is a brilliant as well as a cheap way of minimizing the damage but even in conjunction with a good diet, it is not a complete healthy alternative to quitting. Exercise does not mean that smoking is OK, only that some of the damage is being redressed.

Of course, it is not only smokers who can benefit from moderate exercise or an improved diet.

CHAPTER 11
Tales of smoking and quitting

Ed

Ed was 15 when he started. "I did it for social acceptance – to be one of the crowd – it looked a cool thing to do. I smoked sporadically for a few years, up to ten a day at the most. I gave up because it was disgusting. I was driving along one day, having a smoke, and I thought, 'Damn me, my eyes are smarting' so I threw it out through the window. Bloody-mindedness is what made me give up – all my mates said I couldn't do it, so I did. They used to leave cigarettes about to tempt me and I used to cut them up into little bits and stick notices on them saying 'This is no longer a health hazard'.

"The positive side to smoking was getting away with it, being one of the lads. I never really considered the nuisance value to others, though respect for my parents made me keep it out of home. Cost wasn't an issue and neither was health – at that age, you're immortal – it's never going to get you.

"The negative side was the way I stank and the tarnished fingers and teeth. I didn't like snogging girls who smoked and I thought if I smell like that, I'm stopping.

"I never think deeply about advertising but I do remember someone back in the early 80s showing me some hidden symbolism in Marlboro packs – black and gold discs and broken crosses, and KKK in the pack design. They were supposed to be anti-Semitic and racist. Devious beggars".

Lucy

Lucy, now in her early 30s, smokes more than Ed did. "I was living with a smoker and I just tried it (I was 23) and now I'm hooked! First thing in the morning it's a nice feeling and I think it helps me keep my weight down. If I weren't smoking I'd be eating or chewing my nails.

"I smoke 15–20 a day; I limit myself to 20 per day and if I go over this – say at New Year – I'm really disgusted with myself. The cost isn't really an issue but if I was on the dole I'd try to give up.

"I did give up a couple of years after I started. I was driving along and lit up and then I just thought 'this is disgusting'. I threw it out through the window. I started smoking again 8–10 months later when I was made redundant. I know it's bad for me but I still do it. It needs a lot of willpower to give up. I would definitely give up if I was planning to get pregnant – like at least six months before the pregnancy.

"I'm very conscious of other people – I'll avoid smoking near non-smokers, even in restaurants. I'll also ask other people not to smoke on buses and trains.

"I don't take much notice of the ads. Some of them are very clever, though. They should definitely go on sponsoring sports, like Formula 1 – there wouldn't be any without the sponsorship money".

George

George took up smoking at the age of 25. "I remember vividly my first cigarette. I was in the army – it was Berlin, in January, and we were on the border. It was cold, twenty degrees below zero, and a soldier offered me a cigarette. It was glowing red in his hand and looked lovely and warm and I thought, 'I'd like one of those'. I accepted odd ones over the next three months and then bought my own pack.

"That was 25 years ago. I smoke a pack of 20 in about three days, though I smoke more when I'm bored. I never smoke at home, because my family hate it – I have an old chair in the shed, or smoke in the garden when the weather's good. At work, we've got a smoke-hole to go to.

"I've never tried to give up. I've always been fit and healthy, so I can't convince myself it's bad for my health. Positive effects? Enjoyment, plus when I'm under pressure, it gives me a little thinking time. It seems to have a clarifying effect on the mind. The negative ones are its impact on others. I am aware that my breath goes sour, so I clean my teeth a lot and suck mints.

"I'm not consciously aware of advertising. Under pressure, I'll smoke any brand, though I can't smoke cigars or a pipe".

Maggie

Maggie started in her late teens but was soon smoking 20 a day, to the dismay of her mother, who used to count the butts in the ashtray; she was the only smoker in the family. She continued smoking until she bought her first house. "I couldn't afford the mortgage and the cigarettes – it was as simple as that. I really wanted that house, so the smoking had to stop. I went to a hypnotist but I came out thinking 'that was a real con'. I was giving a friend a lift to work and she lit up the next morning in the car and, to my amazement, it did nothing at all for me! I had no problems stopping but in the end it's the determination that counts. I was terribly constipated for a while; normally, a trip to the loo would be the response to the first cigarette of the day but after stopping, nothing . . . Apart from that, there was no trouble at all. I didn't even put on any weight. I would see in my mind a kind of placard saying 'smoking' briefly once a day but that was all. I never went back and that was about 17 years ago now. I feel like a complete non-smoker."

Rob

Rob started much younger, at the age of 11 with odd cigarettes. By 13, he was smoking 10 per day and the habit grew to 30. "I started because everyone else was doing it and then (1969) it wasn't commonly known as dangerous. I was at boarding school and I had a weekly sub – pocket money.

"I gave up at the age of 23. I was in the Merchant Navy and they were cheap, so cost wasn't an issue, but I was very worried about health – it's such a terrible habit, an addiction. My girlfriend

. . . hurled them out of the porthole

disapproved, too, and one day a friend remarked 'that's a nasty cough'. I was getting through three packs a day, with other people scrounging them. There were no positive aspects – I was purely and simply hooked. There's this horrible smell, everything stinks and there's fag ends everywhere. When I was on watch (4 hours) I'd smoke 15 – smoking two thirds of each cigarette.

"I had two cartons in my cabin, 400 cigarettes, and I hurled them both out of the porthole and said 'That's it'. A mate of mine was a help. He smoked a bit, but he really didn't like it, and we both gave up. It was bloody hard. It gave me problems for 5 years. Even now I sometimes have the odd dream of starting again – it's nightmarish – a warning.

"I remember on leave, three of us were fishing on a small trawler and the other smoker and I ran out of cigarettes. We were winding each other up till we were so desperate for a fag, we made the skipper put in to port. We leaped ashore before he'd tied up, and raced up the hill like lunatics, looking for a shop. We ripped the packing off before we'd even paid for them.

"It's such a precious thing, that pack in your pocket. I'm so glad now that I've given up. I'm just so glad."

Jean

Jean started even younger. "I had my first puff at about 8 years old. Granddad used to smoke rollups and he'd give me a go. He had this machine for rolling them. It had like a hammock thing made of blue material. You put the paper and the filter in, and the tobacco, and sort of pushed it. The hammock rolled over and out popped the cigarette, all made. I used to roll five for him and get one free for me. When I was about nine I remember puffing at my friend's mum's dogends. I first bought my own when I was 11. They were No. 6 – made me go all dizzy and funny. It was something we all did, round the back of school at lunchtime.

"There were no restrictions then. You could buy an individual cigarette and match – they cost 3d (just over 1p). Mum and Dad never knew definitely till I was 18 that I smoked, but I think they sort of knew. I don't smoke much – about 20 a week – and I can go for days without having one."

Paula

Paula, now retired, is a heavy smoker. She suffers from stomach ulcers and is a restless, nervy type. "I started when I was 33 – my husband smokes a pipe – but I wasn't inhaling. I did give up once, about 10 years ago. I just stopped cold but 2 years later I started again. Now I smoke about 40 a day. I couldn't give up, not now."

Ann

Ann was the exact opposite as a smoker. She had her first cigarette at the age of 15, at Christmas. It was given her by her parents. "It was a Sobranie Cocktail. They were very smart – a gold tip and a choice of pretty pastel colours. I never did inhale. It was total posing – I only ever smoked at Christmas or to impress people. I only smoked regularly when I was working for Gallaher, about 10–20 a week, but there were always plenty about for staff to smoke and it was still only social smoking.

"I was totally tolerant of other people smoking. Then I got married and my husband smoked, and living with a smoker I realized what a silly habit it was. I stopped myself – didn't even notice giving up. Then when I was pregnant I suddenly got furious about other people smoking and I even moved offices at work because I couldn't stand the chap I shared offices with smoking. I got really cross at my leaving do when he came and sat beside me and smoked.

"My husband hasn't given up completely but he only smokes outdoors or in a room with the doors shut and all the windows open. We are very careful not to let the smoke get near the children. They know Daddy smokes and talk about 'Daddy's silly habit'."

Clay

Clay started in his late teens, "because I had money in my pocket, because of peer pressure, because it looked cool. I was smoking easily 40 a day. I didn't reckon it was affecting my health but health was a strong reason for giving up. I gave up basically by cold turkey. I bought a bike, kept it quiet that I was giving up and when I felt desperate I just pedaled like fury. Even my girlfriend didn't notice for a few days.

"It was worst at the two-month mark but I gave up for more than five years. Then I started smoking cigars, just one per week. Now I smoke at least one daily but I'm trying to give up again now.

"I have always supported the anti-smokers, especially at work. I think all tobacco advertising should be absolutely banned – I feel very strongly about this. I think it's a good move that the test cases suing tobacco companies are succeeding. Of course, they're not too worried about declining number of smokers in Western countries. They're targeting emerging nations, with phenomenal success."

Judy

Judy is an unusually light smoker; despite having smoked on and off for 30 years, she only smokes about one per week, plus the odd drag from her partner's cigarette, and has never smoked more than five or six per day. She started with a friend out of curiosity, "two teenage girls together".

"Health was never an issue but if I'd been a heavy smoker it would have been. I had a boyfriend whose parents were heavy smokers and they had obvious chest problems. It annoys me when other people smoke – gets on my nerves!

"The positive side of smoking is that it is very enjoyable. It eases social tension – there's a sharing ritual and in acute stress it's comforting. It's also very nice when celebrating, or at a time of excitement.

"I think the morals of the tobacco companies and Governments are appalling. Advertising is bad, especially in Third World countries. Tax revenue on tobacco is vast, so there's no way the Government" (pre-May 1997) "are going to do anything effective to limit consumption. If I were the share-buying sort (which I'm not), I wouldn't buy shares in tobacco companies – but they do provide employment for people."

Rick

Rick is 34, smokes 30 a day, feels fit and healthy, has 'the blood pressure of an athlete' and doesn't want to give up, although he would like to be a non-smoker. He has an active life, on the move all day at work and out in the evenings with his dogs or his gun. "I started at the age of 14 or 15 and bought them out of paper round money and the like. I did it because other kids were doing it. I enjoyed it – still do – but my wife doesn't like it and the kids moan about it all the time.

"I did give up, about two and a half years ago. I'd tried everything – acupuncture, nicorette chewing gum, patches, hypnotism – spent a fortune on hypnotism – and none of it worked. Then one day I'd been out all day, smoked a lot and smoked a lot more in the van on the way home. I was just sick of it and I stopped. I didn't smoke again for nearly eighteen months but I put on an awful lot of weight and I felt bad – heavy and tired. I used to eat all the time. As well as my three full meals, I'd eat a pork pie and maybe a pasty as well, and chocolate all the time, fizzy pop, anything. If I was out in the van, I'd nip into the newsagents and buy a couple of quid's worth of chocolate and I'd eat the lot in the next few miles. I'd feel sick and think, 'why on earth did I eat all that?'.

"I'd had a bad day one day and someone was smoking and I had one too, and I really liked it. It helps me think when I'm busy and rushing and I've lost the weight again – never bother about sweets now.

"I tried low tar cigarettes for a while but they're awful to smoke. You have to suck hard on them and you smoke more. I wasn't enjoying them at all, so I went back to the others.

"I don't want to give up – I'm not ready to. I don't like the smell on my clothes and my breath, but health has never worried me and neither has the cost. I know it's bad for me, of course. I never think about advertising or sponsorship – I'm just not aware of it.

"I knew a chap – farmer – smoked a hundred a day all his life. Unfiltered, and he smoked them down till there was nearly nothing left, then he'd light the next off the stub. The cigarette was never out of his mouth – he didn't hold it in his hand at all. He died at the age of 80 but it was lung cancer.

"I know someone else who was a heavy smoker. He got cancer of the throat and was offered massive surgery, or radiotherapy with a 50/50 chance of success. He didn't fancy the surgery, so he had the radio. He was dreadful – went down to about seven stone – but he smoked all the way through. I went to see him in hospital once and found him outside on a bench, having a fag. That was years ago now and he's completely cured. He still smokes, though not as much as he did."

Laura

Laura is a scientist, now at the peak of her career. She grew up in Communist Eastern Europe and got drawn into smoking when she began working in a lab, because everyone smoked; it just seemed a natural thing to do.

"I had my first smoke when I was seven. I had a friend who was much, much older than me – she was nine – and she said 'I know how to smoke. Come on and I'll teach you', so we went out into the fields during the lunch break at school and we sat down in the long grass and made a cigarette out of leaves and we lit it and smoked it. It was horrible! I decided 'never again'.

Later that day I was called in by the deputy head and asked if I had been smoking but I wouldn't admit to it. It was a very long interview. He said that I had been seen and that my friends had admitted that they were smoking but even when my parents were called in (they worked at the school as well), I still wouldn't admit to it. Later that evening, though, my mother asked me again and I said yes. I didn't mind telling her at home but I really didn't want to confess at school.

"Later, at the age of 17, I tried my first cigarette with tobacco in. I was at a party with a friend and he offered me a cigarette but I found it very unpleasant. Eventually, though, surrounded by smokers in the lab, I did take it up. Before long I was smoking two packs a day. It was too much and I was getting a lot of headaches. Then my PhD supervisor bet me a bottle of champagne that I couldn't give up for a year. For the first month it was very hard indeed. I began to see cigarettes floating in front of my eyes and to dream about them. I sang a lot, folk songs and the like, and I used to seek out smoking friends to sing with, so I was surrounded by this lovely smell. I became an active passive smoker. After a month it began to get easier and I really had no more trouble at all until a week before the year was up, when I suddenly began to see them before my eyes again. The final day was desperate but I made it! As we were drinking the champagne in the lab, I asked someone to give me a cigarette. I found it unpleasant but I started properly again the next day.

"When I came to work in a lab in Cambridge, far fewer people smoked and I tried very hard to cut down. I got down to one or two a day but I did it by having an unlit cigarette in my mouth all the time.

"A few years later I really did stop. I was getting headaches all the time and I had grown older and wiser and at last understood that it was harming me. I told no-one that I was giving up – I just did it.

"My husband did the complete opposite. He went round telling all his friends that tomorrow he would stop smoking. As he said, 'I have promised. How can I break my promise to all these people?' This was what gave him the determination to stop."

Val and Adrian

Val and Adrian (20 and 19) both started smoking at school and both for the same reason: to be in with the crowd. They were 'three a day' smokers – one at morning break, one at lunch time and one in afternoon break, in common with a fair proportion of their classmates. At 13, Val had no trouble buying packs of cigarettes with her pocket money. When Adrian started at 15, he bought cigarettes and got served in pubs: "I always looked older than my age".

Val now smokes 4–5 a day, has tried several times to quit, but only smokes when everyone else is smoking, never with non-smokers. She finds smoking "disgusting and expensive" but smokes for social reasons and very much for stress relief, despite disliking the smell on her breath and clothes.

"The adverts really make it easy for children to get hooked. Benson and Hedges have these leaflets that come through the post – you send off a coupon and get a free lighter – the coupons are freepost, so it doesn't cost anything at all, and you get the free lighter just for sending it in."

Adrian smokes 5–6 a day now, mainly down the pub with friends, having a few drinks. He gave up once for 6 months and didn't really miss it, then one day he was having a drink with friends who were smoking and he just started again.

"I'd like to give up. I'm nowhere near as fit as I used to be and it costs far too much. I used to run half marathons but I can't be bothered now because I'm smoking. It's too much effort.

"The smell is horrible; the smell of the car – if you smoke in the car it gets really disgusting. The house smells horrible, disgusting. The wallpaper gets dirty, your hands go yellow.

"Adverts have nothing to do with it. It's all peer pressure. They could do more with advertising the health risks. The warning on the pack is no use at all – you've already bought it then and you're not going to pay any attention to it."

Kev and Paul

Kev is 19, smokes 20 a day and had his first when he was 13. "It was a Marlboro. I didn't like it at all but smoking just happened. My mates smoked and I started properly when I was 15. I was a 'three a day' smoker. I smoke Embassy now. I'll smoke anything but Marlboro. Yes, I'd like to give up – if it was possible. I've given up loads of times. Nothing works, not even the info lines. I'll smoke for ever – I'll probably die with a cigarette in my hand."

Kev's friend Paul is 17. He's not a smoker – never tried it. "I'm Mr Innocent. I'll never start. I've seen what it did to my Dad. He was in hospital when I was in my second year and it shook me up. He had a faulty heart valve. He gave up smoking back in the 70s but it caught up with him eventually. I have friends who smoke but I never feel under pressure to smoke myself."

The 9–12-year-olds

The 9–12-year-olds are a very decided group. Not one of them approved of smoking; 'disgusting' was an almost universal reaction.

Helen, 11: "It's a very bad habit. I've never tried and I don't want to. Dad smokes about three a day but he wants to stop. I encourage him to stop and Mum wants him to, too. It's a waste of money."

Helena, 12: "My Dad used to but he's given up for 3 weeks now – no, a month. It's a waste of your life."

Richard, 9: "It's a bad habit. I'm not going to smoke but I sometimes see cigarette ads on TV."

James, 10: "It's a bad habit – it damages your body".

119

Stephen, 12: "Disgusting. No-one at home smokes. I never see ads and I'm not going to smoke."

Robert, 10: "Bad for your health. Dad smokes but he's got Nicorette now. I help him – he's going to stay stopped."

Jane, 11: "It's disgusting. My granddad had millions of heart attacks cos he smoked. He died of it."

Tom, 11: "Bad for you. No-one at home smokes but my uncle smokes two a day. He's trying to give up and he's succeeded. I like the smell of it, but I hate it."

Nicola, 11: "I don't like that. I had asthma cos Dad smoked but he gave up about three years ago. It's better now he's given up."

16-year-olds: Alec and John

However, Alec, now 16 and smoking about five a day laughed and said, "yes, I remember saying I'd never smoke when I was that age". He first tried a cigarette when he was 12 or 13. It made him feel adult and he thought it looked good, though he didn't inhale. It was a one-off but he smoked again during an exchange to Italy, because everyone he was with smoked. After finally learning to inhale, he smoked properly for a couple of months and then quit, "though I was having one or two at parties. I began again out of boredom after about a year and I've been smoking regularly for more than 6 months now. It lightens you up – relaxes you. In my class there are about five who smoke properly – the rest can't afford it. There are more girls than boys who smoke at school but they don't smoke as many. Now I'm out of school there's more time to smoke and I value smoking more because of the boredom."

Alec never had trouble buying cigarettes until he was 16, when he was asked for ID and had none on him. He and his friend John reckon it's getting harder for children to buy cigarettes, and they sometimes buy them for younger friends in exchange for a couple for themselves. Cost has never been much of a limiting factor and John would prefer to spend his lunch money on cigarettes and go hungry than eat and go without smoking.

John admits to being dependent on them. "I get moody and shout at my Dad if I haven't smoked for ages" ('ages' turned out to be 4–5 hours) "but I mean to give up. I used to think it was good – cool – but now I just think it's disgusting – I don't like it any more. I had my first cigarette when I was 10. My friend's mum smoked and he stole some off her and told me he'd smoked, so I tried one. We told all our friends and they stole some too; we were all mates smoking together. I thought it was good and I felt great about hiding it and buying them illegally. I was refused loads of times but I just got my older brother or friends to buy them, but from my late 14s on I had no trouble.

"My mum's dead against it – her mum died of lung cancer from smoking. I live with mum in the holidays and I'm dead helpful – take the dog for a walk three times a day and I'm always nipping down to the shop for her. Part of why I smoke is boredom. You need it working" (Alec and John have both been fruit picking since exams finished) " – you can't smoke picking, so you smoke like mad in the breaks. I was going to give up the other night but I'd forgotten about it by the morning. I do want to give up, though – I'm definitely going to give up."

15-year-olds: Patricia, Lou and Coral

Patricia, Lou and Coral are three friends, classmates of 15 in a school with an excellent academic record, with GCSEs approaching. Patricia and Lou both smoke, Coral is a determined non-smoker: "My mum and my dad are both smokers and I can see what it's done to them. No way am I going to smoke." They hang around together, claim to drink impressive quantities of alcohol and are not averse to the odd fight against the girls of the rival school "because there's nothing else for us to do. We just want to go out on a Friday and Saturday and have a good time but there's nowhere to go so we hang around in the park."

Over half the class smoke, they reckon: probably 20 of the 33 girls. Amongst Patricia and Lou's immediate crowd, buying of cigarettes is often communal. "Someone buys a pack and then everyone crashes off them, then someone else buys some." They have no problems buying them in the daytime, though late in the evening the off-licences demand ID.

Patricia had her first cigarette at the age of 13, at a friend's house. He was older and a smoker and, as she said with a charming smile, she doesn't remember the cigarette: "vodka really clouds your perception". She smokes mainly on a Friday and Saturday and occasionally in the week if stressed, "but I might smoke 20 with a friend in a night club. Mum didn't know I was smoking, then she found out. She was holding up this Benson and Hedges pack and saying 'what is this, young lady?' My brother smokes Embassy. My older sister used to smoke. She's 26 now and she gave up when she left college and there was no more exam stress. Smoking is a good relaxer and stress reliever but it's also something to do when you go into a room of people. There's this big

121

awkward silence . . . it also stops you from feeling hungry. I get £2 a day for dinner money but I don't eat, I spend it on other things like cigarettes. Stopping the hunger is not a big reason for smoking but it's a sort of added extra."

She doesn't see any health problems with her own smoking: "I've never had a smoker's cough and we're all going to die some day. You might as well enjoy something while you're alive – you could die at any time."

Lou's mum and dad both smoke, "and I was never going to smoke. It was you" (looking at Patricia) "who gave me my first cigarette". Beneath the laughter was a small undercurrent of feeling: concern at her responsibility from Patricia and a ripple of regret from Lou, with Coral firmly insisting "we're not going to have this conversation". Lou has been smoking for a year now, "generally with friends or sometimes out in the garden. I get an allowance but I spend it mostly on books, but some on cigarettes and alcohol. My parents don't know – well, they don't admit that they know. Mum gave up once for 2 years, then she left her partner and started again."

"The warnings on the packs are stupid. No-one is going to take any notice of that when they've just paid £2.70 or whatever – once you've bought it, you won't throw it away. Superkings have these really stupid slips of paper in the box with advice on how to avoid lung cancer, like not dragging too hard or something. It's like they're advertising against themselves."

Patricia sees herself as smoking for ever more because as far as she is aware it's not doing her any harm: "aren't there some types of cancer that smoking actually cuts down the risk of?". Lou is not so sure; she has a slight cough. (Later, discussing the scientific evidence on smoking and cancer, all three were somewhat taken aback at the real situation.)

On the subject of smoking-related discussion and education, the girls were unanimous. Patricia said, "We had one hour's lesson on smoking about 6 months ago but it was part of the whole respiratory system. I remember that tar coats your lungs and nicotine gets to your brain in 7 seconds, but that's about all.

"It's as if smoking was a taboo subject, at school and at home. They don't want to talk to us about it . . . they don't even want to admit that it's happening."

APPENDIX I

The respiratory and circulatory systems in greater detail

1. The respiratory system

Germs on hang-gliders

1.1 Coughs and colds

When a non-smoker sneezes, out comes a shower of water droplets and mucus. When the sneeze is caused by a cold, the shower will be covered in the cold viruses currently living in the airways. Anyone close at hand is a potential new home for the viruses, but only briefly. Most of what escapes plummets quickly to the ground and the water droplets evaporate, leaving the viruses sinking to earth where their chances of infecting anyone else are pretty small.

When a smoker with a cold sneezes, out come not only the damp bits but a cloud of smoke particles, also covered in viruses. They float around like any other smoke, airborne for a hundred times as long as the non-smoker's viruses: plenty of time to find other noses to breed in.

As well as being highly effective spreaders of respiratory infections, smokers are more susceptible to coughs and colds (though many individual smokers would dispute this) and the effects they suffer are worse. How smoking does this is tied up with how it causes bronchitis and emphysema.

1.2 Bronchitis

Adding 'itis' to anything describes it as inflamed, i.e. red, sore and possibly infected. Bronchi are the tubes through which air flows in and out of the lungs. Bronchitis sufferers are prone to chest infection, cough a lot and have difficulty breathing, and these effects are clearly related to the structure and workings of the bronchi and the damage done to them by smoke.

The bronchial tubes are held open by stiff rings of cartilage (gristle) in their walls. The walls are muscular and can constrict under certain circumstances, for example during an attack of asthma. The inside is covered with a layer of clear, sticky liquid called mucus.

1.2.1 Airways: cleaning up the air

The airways, which include the nose and throat as well as bronchi and bronchioles, pass air in and out of the lungs, warming and humidifying it as it comes in. In addition, they have to deal with potentially harmful air contents such as dust, irritants and pathogens. Large particles are stopped by the hairs lining the nose but smaller items can get into the bronchi.

Imagine the incoming breath full of dust particles. As soon as the particles touch the walls they stick fast to the mucus. Dust doesn't get far down the bronchi before it sticks to the mucus and begins to be carried back out, though the smaller the particle the greater is its chance of getting fairly deep. Most things small enough to get into the alveoli are also small enough to be mopped up and disposed of by phagocytes and removed via the bloodstream.

Many of the pathogens likely to cause trouble in the airways are viruses. When they stick to the mucus, they start to burrow down through it, towards the lining of the bronchi. Viruses responsible for colds and coughs get inside the cells to start breeding and they cause much disruption to the airway lining.

However, the mucus contains antibodies, so if the virus is an old enemy there will be antibodies ready to deal with it. Unrecognized viruses are taken to the lymph nodes, the workshops of the immune system. In a few days, the immune system has made antibodies for the new virus, capable of identifying and either killing them or marking them to be killed by phagocytes, but in the meantime the host has suffered a cold or cough.

The dust and the dead pathogens, trapped on the mucus, move slowly but surely up the bronchi towards the outside. This movement is against gravity while we are upright, so it must be driven by some mechanism.

The surface of the bronchi under the mucus is covered with cilia, microscopic finger-like projections. They move in a coordinated way to make a wave that pushes the layer of mucus up the tubes. When mucus gets to the throat it is usually swallowed for processing with the rest of the food, or can be coughed out of the mouth. The very acid stomach contents kill most pathogens still alive, and the highly alkaline conditions just beyond the stomach finish off the majority of those left.

1.2.2 How good are the defences?

We carry antibodies for every cold we have had but there are plenty of different ones around at any time for us to catch, which is why we keep getting them.

Despite this, the protection provided by mucus, antibodies and cilia is so good that, in healthy people, by the time air gets to the bronchioles it is sterile and fairly clean. However, most of what comes out of cigarettes is in the form of very tiny particles or vapour: all components of smoke can reach any part of the lung.

1.2.3 Effects of smoke on the airway defences

Compared with those of a non-smoker, the smoker's bronchi are darker and narrower: darker because the smoke makes the mucus mucky, and narrower because there is more, and thicker, mucus. This cuts down the space for the air to flow through, so breathing takes extra effort.

There are fewer antibodies in the mucus. This is an important gap in the defences, meaning more infections, which take longer to go and generally include coughing among their effects; more hard work and discomfort.

Healthy cilia, exposed to tobacco smoke, instantly wilt and slow down. Formaldehyde, acetaldehyde and acrolein, all present in cigarette smoke, are particularly potent inhibitors of ciliary movement.

In a long-term smoker, the cilia are almost completely paralysed, to the extent that they cannot move the mucus effectively. This means it has to be coughed out. In more recent recruits to smoking in whom the cilia are less damaged, incoming smoke, even a single drag, has a noticeable paralyzing effect.

When a long-term smoker gives up, unless the cilia have been completely destroyed by smoking, the paralysis fades and, for the next few months, more mucus than usual is produced and carried up to be swallowed or coughed out. The residual coughing and constant throat-clearing makes such smokers reckon they are worse off after quitting, but this is a transient phase.

1.2.4 Smoke irritates and constricts the bronchi

Some of the components of smoke, including those which paralyze the cilia, have a directly irritant effect on the linings of the bronchi, which makes them over-sensitive to normal stimuli, so the slightest thing sets off coughing. The bronchi can even go into spasm, rather like an asthma attack, and constrict. As the resistance to air flow increases (narrower airways), higher driving pressure is needed to force the air in and out. As the problem gets more severe, breathing is laboured and wheezing occurs.

1.2.5 Chronic bronchitis

The combined effect of all this damage is chronic bronchitis, i.e. bronchitis which has become permanent. Bronchitis leads to excessive coughing which is hard work and can be painful. It also makes breathing difficult and leads to infections and tissue damage. It puts a noticeable limit on the amount of exercise which is possible.

As infection gets worse, patches of infected bronchi can rot and smell foul. In extreme cases, the infection can even spread via the blood and form secondary abscesses, particularly in the brain.

1.2.6 Can the damage be repaired?

The way to improve matters is to give up smoking. In recent smokers, quitting allows the body to heal the injuries caused by the smoke. In people who have smoked for a long time, the damage can be too great to be completely repaired.

1.3 Emphysema

The word emphysema is Greek and means 'bodily inflation'. It is a disease of the alveoli and finest bronchioles, in which their walls are weakened and lose elasticity. Emphysematous areas not only fail to function, they prevent surrounding areas from working properly.

1.3.1 Lung tissue elasticity

When breathing out, the elasticity of alveoli helps to expel the air. However, any diseased parts lacking elasticity cannot expel their air.

If the lungs were not held inside the fairly rigid chest cavity, the healthy alveoli would collapse completely and, just like balloons, the initial bit of reinflation would be hard work. The rigidity of the chest cavity limits the emptying of the alveoli, but they can empty a bit more into any nearby areas of emphysema, keeping these over-inflated. Healthy alveoli can even fully collapse into a sufficiently large emphysematous area. As the state of the tissue worsens, the large diseased cavities grow at the expense of nearby small healthy ones. A bronchiole and all its alveoli, having lost elasticity, can end up as one large over-inflated space.

Emphysema tends to develop in discrete areas rather than uniformly throughout the lung. As a damaged area stays inflated during exhalation, it has little influx of fresh air with the next breath. It is thus a non-useful bit of lung volume in itself but, because it tends to be over-inflated, it squashes the neighbouring bits of lung. This makes them less effective, and widespread emphysema can even interfere with the efficient working of the muscles of breathing, the diaphragm (across the base of the chest cavity) and intercostals (between the ribs).

1.3.2 Nitrogen dioxide and emphysema

Nitrogen dioxide is a damaging component of cigarette smoke, though we owe our knowledge of its effects partly to farming. When grass is fermented into silage, enough nitrogen dioxide is produced to reach dangerous concentrations inside the silo. 'Silo-fillers disease' is the name given to the damage caused by breathing it in. It is deadly at surprisingly low concentrations; 90 parts per million, breathed for 4 hours, gives only a 50/50 chance of survival.

It is irritant to lung tissue, causing oedema (swelling) as fluids are drawn from the blood into the tissues which make up the walls of the alveoli and the blood vessels. This not only decreases the space available for air in the alveoli, restricting the quantity of oxygen in the lungs, it also means that the oxygen and carbon dioxide have further to diffuse to move between air and blood. This takes time, so gas exchange is less complete by the end of the breath.

Exposure over a long time to low levels of nitrogen dioxide produces the structural damage seen in emphysema. Nitrogen dioxide definitely contributes to the damage in smokers' lungs, but other substances play a part too. It is not clear how much of the effect of these substances is direct, and how much is due to their provocation of inflammatory phagocytes, which play a big part in smoking-related disease.

1.3.3 Inflammatory phagocytes

These are single cells, capable of complex tasks but also possessing considerable destructive power.

Inflammation is the term which describes an injured or infected area becoming red and hot (extra blood flow), swollen (fluid moving from blood to tissue) and tender or painful (raised tissue pressure and chemical stimulation of nerves); the sensation is familiar to anyone who has had a sore throat, boil or grazed knee. Inflammation is part of the healing process, and is brought about partly by the actions of these cells. Since all phagocytes in the human body are inflammatory, the name phagocyte is sufficient to identify them. However, the term 'inflammatory phagocytes' is used to emphasize their inflammatory potential, which is what, out of control, mediates a fair proportion of smoking related disease.

The inflammatory phagocytes are an army of freely moving defence, repair and maintenance agents. They are carried in the blood in a fairly inactive state, and are part of the white cell population. They help bring about inflammation by releasing chemicals which open up gaps in the walls of tiny blood vessels and squeezing through to the affected tissue. Gaps also allow proteins and extra fluid out of the blood vessels and into the tissues, making the area swollen. Inflammatory phagocytes can be found anywhere in the body, organizing repairs and helping the immune system fight invading pathogens. They carry enzymes capable of liquefying tissues, which they use on pathogens and damaged body tissues. Spilled in the wrong place, these enzymes cause a lot of damage.

Macrophages and neutrophils

There are two groups of inflammatory phagocytes, macrophages (whose name means 'big eaters') and microphages ('small eaters'). The macrophages tend to eat debris, dead cells, old blood clots etc., but also do some organizing of the growth of new tissue. They carry a range of chemical tools to help them clean up and digest damaged tissues, signal to other cells and even kill the odd pathogen.

Microphages specialize in eating and killing invading pathogens. One group, the neutrophils (whose name indicates the kind of dye needed if they are to be seen down a microscope: they will hold a dye of neutral acidity), is particularly important to smokers.

The lungs have their own population of macrophages whose job it is to keep the alveoli clean. This they do by, for example, removing

Repairs

any small particles which get that far, and their presence in lungs is essential. However, healthy lungs contain very few, if any, neutrophils.

Getting angry

Off duty, inflammatory phagocytes are fairly inactive. However, when they sniff an injury or infection they get excited and start releasing chemicals to loosen the junctions between the cells of capillary walls so that they, and other materials for the repairs, can get out of the blood into the tissues. They also release chemicals which call other inflammatory phagocytes and get them excited too. Fully active inflammatory phagocytes are described as 'angry'.

Neutrophils: first on the scene

At the site of an infection, the neutrophils are first on the scene. They specialize in eating and killing bacteria and in digesting debris (dead cells and tissues) to a liquid form. They do this with an array of enzymes they carry. Enzymes are proteins which provoke and hasten chemical reactions without being directly involved, i.e. they are catalysts. Neutrophils are rather short-lived, lasting a few days in the

Getting angry

blood and only hours once they have left the blood and arrived at the site of infection or injury. As they die, they spill their enzymes, thus digesting themselves as well as surrounding tissues.

Macrophages: cleaning up

Once the invading pathogens are under control, the macrophages take over and set about cleaning up and restoring normal function. Macrophages last much longer than neutrophils, their lifetime being months or even (for example in the lungs) years. Where repairs are needed, macrophages release chemicals which control growth in a range of tissues, starting them growing then stopping them again when the repair is complete. They also eat away the old blood clots and debris. They can even direct new blood vessels to grow into an area needing extra blood, for example an injury site undergoing repair.

Chemical weapons

To do all these jobs, the inflammatory phagocytes carry a large range of extremely potent chemicals. They are aggressive fighters, which is fine when they have invading pathogens to kill or dead tissue to digest, but an angry inflammatory phagocyte in the wrong place is capable of doing a lot of damage.

1.3.4 Inflammatory phagocytes in smokers' lungs

Measurements of lung fluids show that regular smokers have about twice as many inflammatory phagocytes as do non-smokers but this hides the fact that, in addition to a near doubling of the macrophages, there are now neutrophils present. Experiments have demonstrated that the smoke-angered macrophages call in the neutrophils. Both can release the enzyme (elastase) which digests elastic tissue, but the neutrophils have about 100 times as much as do the macrophages. As a puff of smoke arrives in the lung, the inflammatory phagocytes become angry and some of them are so badly affected that they burst. Chemical weapons, including elastase and other enzymes, spill out into the alveoli.

The effects are serious. The elastase digests lung tissue. What the inflammatory phagocyte normally uses in careful quantities, to loosen the tightly-closed junction between cells in the capillary wall and make a tiny gap to squeeze through, or to digest harmful pathogens it has swallowed, is sloshing around in the alveolus, weakening its walls, loosening the watertight junctions and thereby permitting oedema. The elastic tissue of the lungs is being eaten away.

Furthermore, in the normal course of events, the odd macrophage will die and spill its contents. The lung protects itself from occasional enzyme spillage with a deactivator chemical which renders the enzyme harmless. In regular smokers, this enzyme deactivator doesn't work properly, leaving the delicate walls of the alveoli and tiniest bronchioles very vulnerable.

1.3.5 Direct chemical damage in smokers' lungs

Oxidation

In the outside world, oxidation is known as rusting, corroding or burning, depending on the exact chemical reaction going on. Cigarette smoke contains many oxidative agents and so do the inflammatory phagocytes, who use them for killing pathogens but also spill them when angry. These oxidative chemicals react with lung tissues.

Anti-oxidants

Lung fluid normally contains vitamin E, one of the anti-oxidant vitamin trio (A, C and E) currently prominent on the chemist's vitamin supplement shelves. In smokers, the concentration of vitamin E, and thus the lungs' protection against oxidation, is reduced, although their blood levels are similar to those of non-smokers. Generous dietary supplements in smokers can raise the vitamin E levels in their lungs, though seemingly not to non-smokers' values. Levels of vitamin E in lung fluid are depleted by smoking, though whether this accounts for all the shortfall is not clear. This depletion leaves the lung tissue open to oxidative damage.

This study is particularly interesting in the light of another (described in Chapter 5 and below) showing reduced levels of vitamin E and selenium in the lungs of both lung cancer patients and members of their families.

1.3.6 Overall damage

The total damage done is a balance between the exposure to smoke and the body's success at repair before the next cigarette. Any coughing and effort of breathing caused by bronchitis increases the damage, by tearing the weakened tissues.

Healthy lungs can supply enough oxygen for strenuous exercise, such as running up several flights of stairs, so most of the time we are only using a little of our lungs' capacity. For this reason, emphysema generally creeps up unnoticed. To smokers who are not in the habit of hard exercise, shortness of breath may not be noticed until about half of their lungs have been destroyed.

1.3.7 Smoking with an infection

Any throat or chest infection will greatly increase the numbers of inflammatory phagocytes in the lungs and airways. Smoking, even passive smoking, with such an infection will multiply the damage done.

1.3.8 Treatment for emphysema

Giving up smoking stops further damage being caused, but the body cannot grow new alveoli and bronchioles to regenerate working lung tissue.

The problems resulting from over-inflation of the emphysematous parts can, in some patients, be alleviated with bronchodilator drugs and physiotherapy. Infections of the diseased tissue are a frequent problem requiring regular antibiotics.

Major open-chest surgery is sometimes performed, particularly in the US, to remove an emphysematous sector of lung, leaving more space inside the rib cage for the working lung tissue. This is called 'lung volume reduction surgery'. However, only a small proportion of patients can really benefit from this technique and, like all surgery, it carries risks.

Ultimately, sufferers from advanced emphysema have such difficulty getting enough oxygen into their blood that they can no longer move freely. Many end their days in a wheelchair, close to an oxygen mask and cylinder, dependent on inhaling aerosols of drugs into their lungs.

1.4 Smoking and environmental respiratory problems

Coal workers can develop *black lung (simple coal worker's pneumoconiosis)*, due to inhaling tiny particles of coal dust. The particles are taken up by alveolar macrophages, the phagocytes routinely found in the lungs, which then get stuck to alveolar walls. Surprisingly, chest x-rays can show simple pneumoconiosis in workers free of symptoms; at this level it affects neither lung function nor life expectancy. Prolonged exposure (10–20 years) can lead a few of those affected to develop *progressive massive fibrosis (complicated pneumoconiosis)*, a seriously debilitating disease in which areas of lung are replaced by black rubbery fibrous tissue, sometimes with cavities full of black fluid. At any level of pneumoconiosis, smoking makes matters far worse, to the extent that, of miners with simple pneumoconiosis, those who suffer adverse effects are almost exclusively smokers.

Cotton mill workers can develop *brown lung (byssinosis)* from inhaling cotton dust, with similar problems in jute and hemp workers. The bronchi rather than the alveoli are affected, and bacteria in the dust are heavily implicated. Typically, sufferers initially cough and feel chest tightness after a few hours' work following the weekend break, but the condition can advance so that the symptoms are permanent, and proceed to respiratory and/or right heart failure. Smoking adds its own problems, but these seem to be independent of byssinosis.

Coal dust and cotton dust are not the only environmental causes of chest disease. Asbestos, with its involvement in lung cancer, is described below. Many of the other respiratory diseases of current concern, such as farmer's lung, mushroom worker's lung and malt worker's lung, are the result of inhaling mouldy dust. Smoking never helps. Asthma, the result of sensitization in infancy to the faeces of house dust mites, which live predominantly on mouldy flakes of human skin in bedding, is a particularly severe problem in many children as well as adults, and asthma attacks can be provoked by smoking, active or passive.

1.5 Lung cancer

Lung cancer was an extremely rare disease before people took up smoking. Of all cancers it is now the biggest killer, in both men and women.

In the US, annual male deaths from lung cancer rose from a very few per 100 000 male population in 1930 to nearly 80 per 100 000 in the late 1980s, at which point it was killing more than three times as many men as either of the next most common cancers, colon/rectum and prostate. Such a dramatic rise excited investigation, with two important papers being published as early as 1950.

Research into the lifestyle of those dying of lung cancer strongly suggested that smoking was the cause. At first, even doctors found it hard to believe; many of them were smokers themselves. Subsequent research confirmed it and, when the news was publicized, smoking among doctors dropped, though the impact on the rest of the population was less impressive.

1.5.1 What is cancer?

Cancer is a disease in which cells, because their genes have been damaged, do not behave like healthy tissue. In particular, they cannot stop multiplying. Groups of cancerous cells can break away and start growing in other places; such lumps are called secondaries or metastases.

The most obvious way in which cancer damages the body is by squeezing other tissues. In lung cancer, airways can be blocked so that air cannot flow, blood vessels squashed so that blood cannot flow and tissues necessary for proper working of the lungs can be pushed aside so that oxygen and carbon dioxide cannot move between air and blood.

Less obvious effects include the release of inappropriate substances from the tumour cells, and these can upset the body in a wide range of ways.

Scientists are finding out a lot about how genes, which control the activity of cells, can be damaged. The story is far from complete but we do know that certain chemicals can react with genetic material. The strands of DNA making up the genes get broken, so the control of the cell goes wrong. Cigarette smoke contains many chemicals capable of damaging DNA and causing cancer.

Cancer is not a single disease but a large collection of diseases which differ with the different types of cell affected. One group of lung cancers, adenocarcinomas, begin in the tiny glands in the lining and appear to have no relationship to smoking. However, they are relatively rare.

1.5.2 Smoking and asbestos

Smoking also increases the risk of getting lung cancer from exposure to asbestos. Asbestos fibres are sufficiently slim to get into the alveoli but too long to be cleared out by the inflammatory phagocytes, so once in, they stay, causing irritation which can eventually progress to lung cancer. The risk of developing lung cancer from exposure to asbestos is far greater in smokers than non-smokers, the combined risk being greater than the sum of the separate risks.

1.5.3 Women and lung cancer

The rise in smoking among women was about 20 years later than amongst men and so was the rise in lung cancer. At around 30 per 100 000 in 1990 it had overtaken breast cancer, till then the biggest cancer killer in women, and lung cancer in women is still climbing steeply.

Lung cancer death curves parallel the respective smoking habits of men and women the world over. In the UK, the male rate has begun to fall, reflecting the impressive decrease in male smoking since the recorded 1948 peak of 82%, down to 28% in 1994. Female smoking peaked at 45% in 1966 and had fallen to 26% by 1994, but lung cancer in women has yet to peak.

Some recent research has worrying news for women. With increased numbers of women dying from lung cancer, it is possible to compare them, and their smoking histories, with men. It seems that women may be more likely (three times more likely in one study) to develop lung cancer than men with the same smoking habits.

1.5.4 Lung cancer, vitamin E and selenium

A Japanese study has shown very reduced levels of vitamin E and of the element selenium in the lungs of lung cancer (including adenocarcinoma, which is not smoking-related) patients. The authors also found that levels of vitamin E and selenium in members of the families of the lung cancer patients were lower than normal, though these family members were not themselves suffering from lung cancer.

As yet, this is just an observation; whether it reflects a direct depletion due to smoking and to passive smoking, poor dietary supply, a link (for example genetic) between lung levels of these two anti-oxidants and susceptibility to lung cancer, or there is some other explanation, remains to be investigated; another topic demanding further research.

Rather like emphysema, lung cancer creeps up unnoticed. Unfortunately, most lung cancer isn't detected until the chance of curing the patient is only one in fifty.

1.5.5 Risks to the individual smoker

The risk of developing lung cancer goes up:
- if the smoker starts young: those who start at 15 years of age are four to five times as likely to die of lung cancer as those who start after 25;
- with the number of years of smoking: smoking for 20 years is 16 times as dangerous as quitting after 10;
- with the number of cigarettes smoked per day: those who smoke 25 or more per day are three times more likely to die of lung cancer than those who smoke fewer than 15 per day, and heavy smokers run a 35 times greater risk than non-smokers.

The risk begins to fall as soon as smoking stops. If lung cancer is going to develop in an ex-smoker, it will most likely do so in the first ten years after giving up. Fifteen years after stopping, the risk of developing lung cancer is only slightly greater than that for a non-smoker.

These statistics relate mainly to males. The situation with females, though not yet clear, is unlikely to be any better.

Nine tenths of cases of lung cancer are caused by smoking and some of the remainder are caused by passive smoking.

2. The circulatory system

2.1 Blood flow and smoking

Inside a normal healthy blood vessel the wall is smooth and, in all but the capillaries, the blood cells glide past the surface without touching it.

The circulatory system works best with smooth flow: if the flow becomes turbulent, for example if the vessel is partially blocked or its wall damaged, not only does the heart have to work harder to pump the blood but there is mechanical wear as cells swirl around and collide with vessel walls. (In the capillaries, which are tiny, blood moves slowly and its cells are in contact with the walls, the red cells

Nicotine makes the heart work harder

unloading oxygen and loading carbon dioxide.)

In normal healthy blood vessels there is a lining layer, the endothelium, of special cells which fit very closely to each other, leaving no gaps. They form a smooth, unbroken 'non-stick' lining, preventing blood clotting on the vessel walls. However, if the endothelium is injured and blood touches the muscular wall behind it, it immediately begins to clot. Clotting stops torn vessels bleeding and allows repairs to begin but is inappropriate when the vessel is not leaking.

Three experimental observations illustrate the effects of cigarette smoking on blood vessels.

First, blood serum from smokers disrupts the healthy endothelium. Serum is the liquid left after blood has clotted, so it has no cells in it, but it carries many of the smoke chemicals. The endothelial cells, which should be joined tightly together, pull apart, leaving gaps and exposing the muscle behind them. With prolonged exposure they begin to die

Second, smokers' blood has more dead endothelial cells in it than does non-smokers' blood, and it also has more phagocytes.

Third, fifteen minutes after a cigarette, flow near the vessel's surface is no longer smooth. White cells from the blood are clinging to the vessel wall, either rolling along it or completely stuck, some singly and others in clumps. The white cells include

137

phagocytes and some have platelets stuck to them (platelets, described below, start the clotting process by becoming sticky).

These tiny but, at this stage, reversible changes are the first steps to death or severe disablement by heart attacks, strokes, gangrene and other diseases. How this happens is tied up with what is in blood, how it clots and how damaged blood vessels are repaired.

2.2 Blood

2.2.1 Healthy blood

Blood is made up of red cells, platelets and white cells floating in plasma, a clear liquid. The difference between serum and plasma is that serum is the liquid obtained by allowing the blood to clot, and plasma is the liquid obtained by physically removing the cells from blood. This means that plasma contains the dissolved proteins which are converted to solid reinforcing fibres during clotting, whereas serum does not. Plasma has only been easy to separate from the blood cells since centrifuges, described below, were invented.

Imagine being able to look down a microscope into a blood vessel in a reasonably healthy adult and watch what flows past. Most of what is visible are the red blood cells. Amongst the red cells there are a few smaller clear discs, but only one for about every 25 red cells going past. These are the platelets. Occasionally a white cell will go past. There are far fewer of these, only one for about every thousand red cells and forty platelets, though their numbers can rise in response to injury or infection.

Red blood cells carry oxygen (when they look bright red) and carbon dioxide (when they look much bluer). They give the blood its colour: red blood coming from the lungs and rather bluer blood going back to them. They are made in the bone marrow.

Platelets start the clotting process to plug wounds. They are not complete cells, as they have no nucleus, but are made by giant cells in bone marrow dividing themselves to give several thousand platelets each.

White blood cells are of two main types:

Lymphocytes (literally, 'lymph cells'), which recognize and fight dangerous pathogens. They, like the antibodies, are made by our immune system. The lymph glands, which are found at many places in the body, swell when they are busy and if the doctor can feel lumps behind someone's ears, he knows they are fighting an infection.

Phagocytes (literally, 'eater cells'), which are the repairers and cleaners of the body. They gather at sites of injury or infection, eat up pathogens and dead tissue and organize the repairs. Like the red cells and platelets, they originate in the bone marrow. Phagocytes are inflammatory cells, i.e. they are involved in causing inflammation, part of the healing process following infection or injury.

Normally, lymphocytes make up roughly one third of the white cells. The two kinds often work together, the inflammatory phagocytes disposing of pathogens killed or captured by the lymphocytes. We can produce lots of extra lymphocytes or inflammatory phagocytes when pathogens invade or injuries occur.

The cells are very small; 10 ml (two teaspoons) of healthy blood contains ten times as many cells as there are humans on earth:

40–66 thousand million red blood cells
1.5–4 thousand million platelets
40–120 million white blood cells

(1997 world population 5.5 thousand million, UK population approx. 60 million)

Plasma is the liquid left if all the cells and platelets are removed. Plasma is basically water, with many different things, including antibodies, repair materials and digested food, suspended or dissolved in it. It can even have oily droplets floating in it after a fatty or oily meal. Plasma is just over half the volume of blood.

The cells are slightly heavier than the plasma, so given time and if clotting is prevented, they sink under gravity. They can settle out in blood vessels where flow is extremely slow, such as leg veins during prolonged inactivity (couch potatoes should keep their feet up). In hospital labs which analyze blood samples, this separation is speeded up by spinning the blood in tubes in a centrifuge, the tubes arranged like spokes in a wheel. Being heavier, the cells rapidly pack themselves at the outer end of the tube and the plasma is all left at the inner end.

2.2.2 Smokers' blood

In smokers, up to 10% (more in very heavy smokers) of the places in red cells for carrying oxygen and carbon dioxide are taken over by carbon monoxide. It is not just a question of the carbon monoxide passively hogging the oxygen transport; its presence alters how tightly the oxygen is held, so when it gets to the tissues some of the oxygen cannot be offloaded. To make up for the poor oxygen supply to tissues, the body produces extra red cells, but they do make the blood thicker and so harder to pump, which means extra work for the heart.

Platelets clot by becoming sticky and clinging together. Smokers' platelets are permanently slightly sticky, making them liable to start clotting where they shouldn't. This is a particular problem where blood flow is sluggish, such as the leg veins in someone standing or sitting still for long periods, and the cells and platelets tend to settle out of what flow there is and clump together, aiding clotting. Smokers' plasma also has extra clotting protein in it, making it thicker and so harder for the heart to pump as well as more prone to clotting.

Smokers have high numbers of inflammatory phagocytes. Inflammatory phagocytes in the lungs are made angry by the smoke and cause damage by digesting lung tissue. The inflammatory phagocytes in smokers' blood damage the walls of the blood vessels.

The endothelium is more than just a non-stick surface. It holds the vessel open by keeping the muscle in the wall relaxed, releases chemicals which control clotting and can, for example when damaged, order extra inflammatory phagocytes. Badly damaged endothelium causes the vessel wall muscle to go into spasm, greatly reducing the flow of blood. Only when the levels of smoke chemicals in the plasma have fallen can things calm down and repairs begin – till the next cigarette.

2.2.3 Normal blood clotting

When someone cuts their finger, it bleeds for a while and then stops. As the injury happens, blood escapes from the severed vessels. The muscles in the vessel walls immediately go into spasm, squeezing them almost closed and reducing the gush to a trickle.

As soon as the platelets get close to the torn edge, they respond to the chemical environment of the cut surfaces by tensing up into balls and developing spiky surfaces, a bit like velcro or goose grass/sticky willie. At the same time, they release a chemical which diffuses through the plasma. As soon as it reaches other platelets, they tense up and go sticky. Soon they are all clinging together and signaling others to come and join them. Before long, the growing plug of sticky platelets fills the gap and the vessel stops bleeding.

Next, a network of fibres appears out of nowhere, threading around through the plug and tying it more firmly together. The threads are fibrin and are being made by a series of chemical changes in fibrinogen (literally 'fibrin generator'), one of many proteins dissolved in plasma.

It is the chemical messengers released by injured tissues and sticky platelets which help to start and build clots. If the blood is flowing too quickly, these chemicals get washed away before they can act. Slowly flowing blood thus clots more readily than quickly flowing blood.

2.2.4 Smoking and clotting

Compared with normal blood, smokers' blood is thicker and more sluggish and the platelets are slightly stickier. The sluggishness is due to extra red cells, produced in an attempt to compensate for the carbon monoxide, and extra fibrinogen produced in response to smoke chemicals. Both of these make the blood thicker and harder to pump. The stickiness of the platelets is due, at least in part, to a factor released from the endothelial cells in response to smoke-laden plasma.

Sticky platelets and slow-flowing blood both encourage clotting, and fibrin reinforcing threads are more readily formed with the extra fibrinogen. Damaged vessel endothelium completes the story, providing plenty of places where clots are encouraged to start. Clots forming inside blood vessels can block the flow of blood.

Although extra clotting might seem like an advantage, normal blood already clots fast enough and in general those whose blood doesn't clot properly, such as haemophiliacs, are lacking a part of the clotting system for which smoking does not compensate.

2.3 Blood Vessels

We have three main sorts of blood vessels.

Arteries carry blood which is at high pressure due to the pumping of the heart. Their walls are thick, made of muscle and elastic tissue, and they distribute blood to the capillaries. The very smallest arteries, just before the capillaries, are called arterioles. Arterioles are the 'taps' used to turn up or down the blood supply to their particular area and they, like arteries though to an even greater extent, are controlled by nerves, by circulating messenger chemicals and by locally produced substances such as the by-products of energy production in muscle. Nicotine, too, can interfere with the control of arteries and arterioles.

Capillaries are tiny thin-walled vessels. They carry blood, moving slowly, into close contact with all body tissues to deliver supplies and take away waste. They are so narrow that the red cells have to roll up slightly to squeeze along them, which puts the oxygen they carry physically close to the tissues which need it. Substances including smoke chemicals in the plasma also pass readily through the thin capillary walls into the tissues.

Veins collect blood from the capillaries and take it back to the heart. Their walls are also elastic and muscular but the blood is at much lower pressure than in the arteries, so their walls don't need to be so thick.

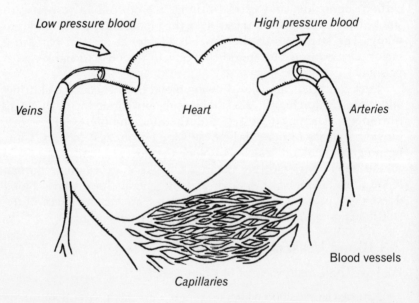

Most of what we know about damage to blood vessels due to smoking concerns arteries and veins, with damaged arteries being the bigger cause of death and disease. This does not mean that smoking doesn't damage capillaries, only that the results of damage are less dramatic. For example, if a major artery is blocked, a whole chunk of tissue, which could be brain or heart, dies; the destruction of thousands of capillaries around the body would be trivial by comparison.

2.3.1 Smoking and damage to arteries

In smokers, the artery walls are likely to have not only gaps in the endothelium but also some dead endothelial cells. The endothelium helps hold the vessel open, by supplying nitric oxide to relax the layers of muscle underlying it. This action is controlled by nerves and by substances circulating in the blood: overall control, such as adrenalin (butterflies in the tummy when frightened), or local control from locally-produced substances, for example by-products of energy production. Any damage to the endothelium interferes with its ability to control the vessel properly, and when it fails totally, the vessel can go into spasm, becoming very narrow.

In established smokers, the artery wall may be swollen and bulging in some places, with some bulges so large and lumpy that they obstruct normal blood flow. Some even have clots growing on them, streaming along the vessel with the flow. This situation has two inherent dangers: first, the clot or the bulge might grow so big that it blocks the vessel, and second, the clot or bits of the damaged, bulging artery wall might break away and block a narrower blood vessel further downstream.

Atheroma

The medical name for these lumpy patches is atherosclerotic plaques, or atheroma. It is not yet clear how these bulges form but they probably begin with damage to the endothelium, which allows things in the blood to invade the wall of the artery.

Inside the lumps are macrophages and fat. Fat is in between cells as well as being inside macrophages and also inside the muscle cells of the artery wall. Whether the macrophages were angry and chewed their way in, or came in to repair the damage and remove the fat which was seeping in, is not clear; probably both.

There is also damaged muscle and elastic tissue, patched up with fibrous connective (scar) tissue, the body's great repair material.

The surface of the bulge is a battleground between endothelial cells constantly trying to grow over and smooth the surface, and more damage, with platelets and macrophages from the blood getting in through gaps. In very severe atheroma, the top can become crusty and break away, or be covered by a clot over which a new layer of endothelial cells grows.

Non-smokers can also suffer from atheroma but smoking definitely increases the risk. For young smokers, the increase in risk is huge. In older smokers, the risk of atheroma from causes other than smoking begins to catch up with the smoking risk.

2.3.2 Smoking is not the only cause of atheroma

Other risks include high blood pressure (which increases the mechanical damage), lack of exercise, a diet over-rich in some things (most famously saturated fat) or poor in some other nutrients, and possibly some pathogens infecting vessel walls. The relationship between atheroma and various kinds of fat in the diet is the subject of much research and as yet not fully understood. High levels of an amino acid called homocysteine are also associated with high risk.

The possible role of organisms such as some of the chlamydiae and cytomegalovirus (a member of the herpes group of viruses) is currently the subject of research. It is suspected that such organisms may find it easier to gain access to the cells of vessel walls which have been damaged by smoke.

2.3.3 Smokers: blocked vessels

The effect of blocking a blood vessel depends on where it is. Smokers are prone to blockages in the following areas (and thus diseases):

Brain (stroke)

The brain is extremely dependent on a proper blood supply and when an artery in the brain is blocked, brain tissue immediately stops working and dies within a few minutes. So far, medical science knows no feasible way of replacing dead brain cells.

The result for the person suffering the stroke can be sudden death or loss of some function. Some of the common disabilities from stroke are loss of speech, paralysis, blindness and loss of memory.

Heart (heart attack)

The muscles of the heart, which pump day and night throughout life, get their oxygen and food from blood vessels which run through them. These are called the coronary vessels.

Coronary arteries are always moving with the action of the heart. They are particularly likely, because of all the mechanical wear and tear, to get damaged and develop atheroma. Any blockage of a coronary artery is likely to lead to a heart attack. The special risks to the heart posed by smoking are described in more detail further on.

Limbs (peripheral vascular disease, gangrene)

Peripheral vascular disease is the name given to blockage of the small arteries or veins in the legs (and very occasionally arms). It is seen mainly in smokers, although it can be a complication of diabetes. The vessel walls are full of macrophages and much of the blood flow is blocked by clots.

The symptoms start with pain on walking but, if the person continues to smoke, the pain becomes more frequent and the legs get weaker. Eventually gangrene sets in. Gangrene is the result of tissues dying through lack of blood supply, and it has no cure. The only way to stop it spreading is to amputate.

Very similar effects result from narrowing of larger arteries to the legs. One way or another, smoking is responsible for the amputation of about 29 legs a week in England and Wales. However, amputation is a treatment of last resort and far more sufferers spend the latter portions of their lives in wheelchairs, to spare what little oxygen can get to the leg muscles for keeping the tissues alive rather than waste it on walking. Milder cases are able to walk no more than a few steps. Talking to any sufferer will reveal that peripheral vascular disease, in addition to severely restricting lifestyle, is a very painful condition.

The lack of oxygen is not only due to the restricted blood supply. What blood can get through delivers less oxygen because it is carrying carbon monoxide.

At this level, other seemingly more marginal of the potentially toxic components of smoke become important. Hydrogen cyanide, the deadly agent used in gas chambers, kills so rapidly because it gets straight into cells and prevents them taking up oxygen and using it to produce energy. Hydrogen cyanide poisoning leads to a cherry-red appearance because the venous blood is still oxygenated.

In the conditions leading to peripheral vascular disease, the added burden of the small quantities of hydrogen cyanide around is an important one: with what scarce supply of oxygen as exists being denied to cells, gangrene is hardly surprising. Hydrogen cyanide is similarly compromising to the brain and heart (indeed, any tissue) when oxygen supplies are restricted. There are plenty of other toxic chemicals in low concentrations, too.

Buerger's disease is a similar but separate condition, confined to very heavy smokers and almost exclusively to men. It involves veins as well as arteries and upper as well as lower limbs. The early stages of the disease are inflammatory, and a hypersensitivity to nicotine or to some other substance in tobacco smoke, as well as a genetic predisposition, have been suggested as possible causes.

2.3.4 Smokers: bursting arteries

The other way in which a vessel can fail is to burst, and this happens in smokers' arteries as a result of weakened vessel walls and high blood pressure.

Aorta (massive internal bleeding)

Most spectacularly, the aorta (the main artery coming out of the left side of the heart) can burst, causing intense tearing pain in the chest, abdomen or back. The blood is generally held in by the tough outer layer of the artery, though it can burst right through and spread into the body. As all the blood in the body is pumped through the aorta in about a minute and a half (less during exercise), death is almost certain. Only about 10% of people with such a burst, known as a ruptured aortic aneurysm, survive.

When the blood stays within the outer layer, or leaks slowly, surgery gives a better chance of survival and if the aneurysm (ballooning) is detected and repair attempted before it starts to bleed, the chances are good. After any kind of leak without surgery, death comes in a few days at most.

For every twelve people dying this way, eleven are either smokers or ex-smokers.

Cerebral arteries (stroke)

Severe damage also results when vessels burst in the brain, causing total or partial brain death, i.e. stroke. The results for the person suffering the stroke are roughly the same whether it is caused by blockage (cerebral thrombosis or embolism) or bursting (cerebral haemorrhage).

2.3.5 Normal action of the aorta

All arteries have elastic walls. The aorta is the biggest of the arteries, and through it flows all the blood coming out of the left side of the heart. The elasticity is an essential feature in distributing the blood around the body, and in particular in getting a blood supply to the heart muscle.

Pressure pulse and blood flow

The pulse spreads along the arteries when the valve between the heart and the aorta opens, travelling through the blood at roughly the speed of sound – far faster than the blood can move. The pulse is the pressure wave generated by the heart, not a slug of blood shooting out of the heart and rushing along the arteries.

The blood spurts from the heart into the aorta but the flow is much steadier further along the arteries.

Elasticity in artery walls smoothes the blood flow

The walls of the arteries, especially the aorta, expand outward a little as the pressure is rising, to take the blood gushing out of the heart. This expansion is within the normal elasticity of the artery, a far cry from the ballooning of an aneurysm. As the heart empties, the pressure falls until a 'bang', one of the more prominent of the heart sounds the doctor listens for with the stethoscope, signals the closing of the valve on the output of the heart.

The elastic artery walls begin to recoil inward again, squeezing the blood on down the artery and, at the same time, stopping the blood pressure in the aorta falling to zero. Zero, in blood pressure terms, means the pressure of the outside world, i.e. atmospheric pressure.

Meanwhile, behind its closed valve, the heart has refilled and is squeezing to raise the pressure inside it. As soon as the pressure in the heart is greater than that in the aorta, the valve opens and more blood comes out. The heart goes on squeezing, so the pressure goes on rising, until it has emptied sufficiently for the pressure to drop, when the valve closes again.

This ability of the artery walls to expand and contract is important; it is what keeps the blood flowing smoothly even though the heart pumps it out in a stop-go manner. It is also the way the artery walls cope with the wear of the continuous pressure pulses. A tube with little elasticity would have to be strong-walled to avoid splitting, a factor familiar to people who design industrial pipework.

Muscle in vessel walls controls the flow

The muscle in the vessel wall acts as a tap to control the flow of blood. Demand for blood flow around the body varies with what the person doing. For example, when running, the leg muscles need lots of blood so arteries to the leg muscles open up. During lunch, the digestive system needs more blood and the leg muscles less, so the digestive system arteries open up and the leg ones close down a bit. Much of the control occurs at the level of the arterioles.

The veins, too, adjust their size to the quantity of blood flowing through them.

2.3.6 Nicotine and blood vessels

Nicotine is at the heart of the whole smoking issue because it is responsible for much of the addictive quality of tobacco. It also affects the heart and blood vessels in a number of ways, the overall effect being to raise the blood pressure and heart rate. It restricts blood flow to the skin by narrowing down the arteries supplying the skin, causing a drop in skin temperature and leading to poor skin condition. To a lesser extent, it narrows down all vessels.

Theoretically, smokers ought to have permanently raised blood pressure and heart rate as a direct result of the nicotine but there is a paradox: as a group, smokers do not suffer from particularly high blood pressure.

To a certain extent, smokers' cardiovascular responses to successive doses of nicotine (obtained by smoking) get smaller as the day wears on, though the first cigarette of the day produces a sharp rise in both blood pressure and heart rate. Furthermore, after abstaining from smoking for a week, their response to nicotine is nearly twice as great as if they had merely not smoked overnight.

This adaptation to repeated doses is known as acute tolerance. Although it means that smokers probably don't respond as sharply to nicotine as would a non-smoker, it seems unable to fully account for the paradox, especially as a feature of withdrawal from smoking is a drop in heart rate and blood pressure. One possibility, discussed in Chapter 9, is that people most likely to become smokers start off with lower than average blood pressure and heart rate so the effect of nicotine is to raise them towards average levels.

Interestingly, the response of the blood flow in the skin to nicotine does not exhibit this acute tolerance, with skin temperature, which falls as the blood flow lessens, directly reflecting the concentration of nicotine in the blood throughout the day.

2.3.7 Low level smoke exposure: a hazard to vessels

Recent advances in ultrasound technology in medicine have made it possible to measure the thickness of arterial walls non-invasively. An increase in the thickness of artery walls reliably reflects hardening of the arteries and is a useful predictor of death from cardiovascular disease.

One study has looked at the effect of smoking on the rate of thickening of arteries in smokers, ex-smokers, passive smokers and non-smokers. Two sets of measurements were made on arteries in the necks of each subject, the second three years after the first. Everyone's arteries thicken as they get older, but in this study the smokers' arteries thickened 50% faster than did those of the non-smokers.

Incredibly, ex-smokers who were still passive smokers did almost as badly, and ex-smokers who were not passive smokers, i.e. they spent less than one hour a week in a smoky atmosphere, still showed a rate of thickening 25% greater than non-smokers. This implies that progressive damage to blood vessels cannot be totally halted by quitting.

Perhaps most worrying of all, non-smokers who were passive smokers (as little as one hour per week) had a 20% faster thickening than did true non-smokers. This has serious implications for all passive smokers, as well as those who feel that the effect of their smoking on others is negligible. What passive smoking does to the arteries of children remains to be established, but it is reasonable to assume, unless demonstrated otherwise, that the effect is harmful.

Arteries are not only narrowed by the thickening of the walls, their walls are stiffer and cannot expand and recoil so well with the pumping of the heart. Within the vessel wall, some of the muscle and elastic tissue has been replaced by connective (scar) tissue, the tough stuff used for so many repairs in the body where the original tissue cannot be replaced. Continual damage due to the invasion of smoke chemicals, macrophages and fat have advanced the ageing of these arteries, making them far less efficient and controllable channels for the delivery of blood. It is also likely that the vasa vasorum suffer blockage. These are the tiny vessels which supply blood to the muscles of the thick-walled arteries. Being tiny, they are easily blocked, with resultant damage to the arterial walls.

With this effect all over the body, delivery of the appropriate quantity of blood, on demand, becomes less and less easy. For the person, activities are limited; no sudden bursts of energy, not much exercise, even a sluggish brain.

2.4 The heart

The heart has some unique features which make it rather vulnerable to the damage smoking can do and explain why smoking is so dangerous for the heart.

The heart has four pumping chambers, two on the right receiving blood from all over the body and pumping it to the lungs, and two on the left receiving it from the lungs and pumping it round the rest of the body. However, it is the left ventricle (the second stage of pumping) which produces the highest pressures, does the most work and has the greatest volume of muscle. It is therefore the most likely to suffer damage.

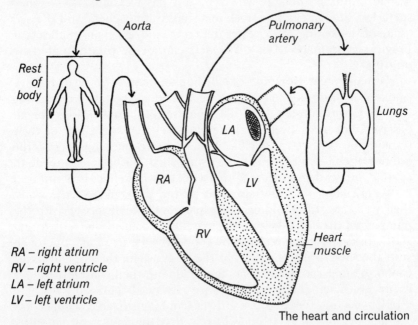

RA – right atrium
RV – right ventricle
LA – left atrium
LV – left ventricle

The heart and circulation

2.4.1 Stop–go coronary blood flow

The heart is made mainly of muscle and like all muscle it needs a blood supply. The vessels running through the heart muscle are called coronaries. They branch off the aorta and the way the blood flows in them is rather surprising . . . it keeps stopping! While the heart is pumping blood out into the aorta, the blood in the coronaries stops flowing and while the heart is filling it moves again.

150

Odd as this looks, the explanation is simple. Everything within the heart is either liquid or softish tissue, so the pressure is going to be very similar everywhere. When the pressure of the blood inside the heart chambers is at its highest, so is the pressure within the muscle surrounding the chambers and so, therefore, is the pressure inside the coronary vessels.

With the pressure equally high in the aorta and all along the coronaries, there is no pressure difference to make the coronary blood flow. However, when the pressure in the heart drops to its zero, the pressure in the aorta is still high because of its elastic walls, and this pressure drives blood along the coronaries. Thus the elasticity of the aorta is essential for supplying the coronary blood flow.

2.4.2 Oxygen extraction

With the blood in the coronaries sitting still and the heart muscle working hard, there is time for most of the oxygen to be extracted from the blood. This is in contrast to other muscles in the body, which only take some of the passing oxygen; if they need a little more, they take more from what is flowing past. They only need to increase the quantity of blood flowing when their requirements rise considerably.

2.4.3 Increased oxygen delivery requires increased blood flow

When the heart has to work harder, it needs extra oxygen. To deliver the heart muscle's extra oxygen supply, the coronaries have to get wider. This is the best way the heart has of increasing its own blood supply. Increasing the peak (systolic) blood pressure does little, because the blood in the coronaries can't flow when the pressure in the heart muscle is high, and though increasing the trough (diastolic) pressure would push more blood round the coronaries, such a rise is incompatible with good health. Increasing the heart rate makes matters worse, because there is less time per beat when the coronary supply can flow.

The problem is solved by the chemical products of the reaction supplying energy to the heart muscle, which act directly on the coronary vessels to open them up, allowing more flow.

2.4.4 Effect of a single cigarette on coronary flow

During some medical investigations of chest pain, which included inserting catheters into the coronary vessels of awake patients in order to look (with x-rays) for any sites of blockage, it was possible to observe the effects of smoking a single cigarette on the diameter of various coronary vessels as well as the rate of blood flow through them. All the patients were smokers.

The effects of smoking were clear. Five minutes after a cigarette, the coronary flow rate had decreased by 7%, despite an increase in oxygen demand due to the increased heart rate and blood pressure. In one very clear set of pictures, what can be seen as a minor narrowing in a coronary artery before smoking became a serious constriction after the cigarette. The muscles in the coronary wall had constricted, but administration of nitroglycerin via the catheter not only relaxed the constricted patch but increased the diameter of the other vessels in the picture. Nitroglycerin is routinely used to treat angina (pain due to restricted oxygen supply to heart muscle) as it rapidly relaxes constricted vessels; not, some may be relieved to hear, in its familiar capacity as an explosive, but by acting unignited on the vessel walls.

Half of the patients in the study had apparently normal, smooth, undamaged endothelium in the coronary arteries examined, i.e. no visible atheroma. The authors of the study noted that there could, nevertheless, be functionally damaged endothelium. Smoking a single cigarette resulted in mildly to severely constricted coronary arteries, and a damaged endothelium was a likely link in the chain.

2.4.5 Carbon monoxide and the heart

Carbon monoxide is felt to be a major contributor to cardiovascular problems, because users of smokeless tobacco (snuff, chewing tobacco etc.), who get no carbon monoxide with their nicotine, are less susceptible to cardiovascular problems. Carbon monoxide cuts down the oxygen available from blood, a serious problem for the heart muscle, and in a long term smoker the blood itself tends to flow more slowly because it is thicker. There is also the possibility that the reduced oxygen level adversely affects the endothelium.

The individually small effects of various smoke chemicals add to the problems caused by carbon monoxide; for example, hydrogen cyanide is the last thing the coronaries or heart muscle needs, even in tiny quantities.

2.4.6 Endothelial damage in the coronary vessels

The coronaries suffer a lot of mechanical wear and tear due to the incessant movement of the heart muscle, so they are more prone to endothelial damage than are other arteries. This leads to difficulty in controling the coronary vessels, because it is the endothelium which produces the nitric oxide which holds the vessel wall muscle relaxed and thus the vessel open.

Damaged endothelium also raises the likelihood of both atheroma and clotting, either of which will further block the vessel.

2.4.7 Heart muscle starved of oxygen

The effects of smoking, both long-term and in immediate response to a cigarette, combine to deprive the heart muscle of oxygen. Like any over-used muscle, the oxygen-starved heart gets painful. Because of some oddities in the way the nervous system is arranged, this pain, which is called angina pectoris, is felt not in the heart but in the chest or left upper arm. The pain is caused partly by a build-up of lactic acid, which is a product of the emergency chemical reaction our cells use to produce energy without oxygen. In most muscles, this is uncomfortable but not serious; the familiar aching muscles the day after hard exercise.

However, the heart cannot stop for a rest. Angina is a warning which needs to be taken seriously. One possible consequence of too much acid building up is that the electrical signal which drives the heart's rhythm is shorted out. The muscle fibres then flutter at random and the heart cannot pump properly. The random fluttering is called fibrillation and its consequences depend on which bit of the heart is fibrillating and, to a certain extent, what triggered the fibrillation.

Ventricular fibrillation, i.e. fibrillation affecting the second stage of pumping on either side of the heart, is a catastrophic event and the excitement of reviving the dying patient with electrical shocks from the defibrillator is a familiar part of television hospital dramas. Real life defibrillation is every bit as dramatic, though its success rate is considerably lower than television drama suggests.

Atrial fibrillation, i.e. fibrillation affecting the first stage of pumping, can seriously affect the filling of the ventricles to the point where the quantity of blood pumped out by the heart is severely reduced without being totally catastrophic, and people suffering atrial fibrillation can carry on reasonably well. What commonly happens is that blood clots within the heart, but prompt medical attention is reasonably effective.

2.4.8 Heart attack

In the most serious heart attacks, a major coronary artery is blocked and the whole heart stops. Ventricular fibrillation commonly, though by no means always, results, but under these circumstances defibrillation is not enough to restore heart function. No blood flows and within minutes the brain is dead.

In less serious heart attacks, narrowing of an artery affects a small patch of muscle, sometimes with the effects building up over a long time, sometimes more suddenly, but the patient survives. The patch of heart muscle dies and is replaced in time by connective tissue – tough enough to take the pressures of the heart but unable to share in the work. The remaining heart muscle has to do all the work, so is more at risk of an attack in the future.

The name for this death of a patch of heart muscle is a myocardial infarct. When it involves the full thickness of the heart muscle, the eventual repair patch is generally thinner than the muscle wall, leaving a little hollow inside the heart where blood can eddy and clots can form: an additional hazard.

Heart attacks can also result from disease of the electrical signal generator but there is no obvious relationship with smoking.

In conclusion

Smoking adversely affects both the respiratory and circulatory systems, causing immediate tissue damage which develops over time into disease: 50% of smokers die prematurely. Despite an impressive decline over the last 25 years in smoking-related deaths among middle-aged Britons, who are heeding the health message and quitting, smoking remains by far the biggest avoidable cause of death. The increasing rate of smoking among those too young to legally do so demonstrates that the health message has a long way still to go.

Appendix II

Glossary

acute: (medical) brief; sometimes used to imply severe

acute tolerance: (to nicotine) a smaller response to successive doses; response restored to full size after a period of abstention

alveoli: tiny elastic air sacs in lung; oxygen passes from alveoli to blood, which surrounds them, and carbon dioxide passes out

aneurysm: ballooning of artery due to weakness of wall

angina pectoris: pain felt in chest or left upper arm due to oxygen shortage in heart muscle

antibodies: special proteins which recognize and combine with, for example, invading germs

aorta: main artery coming out of the left side of the heart; other arteries branch off it

arteriosclerosis: hardening of the arteries

asthma: disease in which bronchi are prone to periods of constriction and swelling, and can have excess mucus, making breathing laboured; generally in response to airborne pollution, exertion or emotion

atheroma: fatty deposits causing swelling on inside of artery wall; can cause blockage

atherosclerosis: arteriosclerosis with atheroma which can be fibrous and hardened

atherosclerotic plaques: atheroma

bronchi: tubes through which air moves in and out of the lungs; muscular, held open with rings of cartilage (gristle)

bronchodilator: drug for dilating bronchi by relaxing the muscle; commonly in inhalable form, used to treat asthma attacks and other problems due to constricted bronchi

bronchioles: tiniest branches of bronchi; no cartilage

bronchitis: inflammation of the bronchi

carcinogen: substance which causes cancer

cardiovascular: involving the heart and blood vessels

cerebrovascular: involving the brain and its blood vessels

chronic: long-lasting or frequently recurring

chronic bronchitis: bronchitis which lasts a long time

chronic obstructive lung disease: (COLD, also COPD, chronic obstructive pulmonary disease): bronchitis and emphysema

cilia: (in bronchi) tiny finger-like projections from bronchial surface which move the mucus up out of the lungs

coronary: involving the blood vessels supplying the heart muscle

cot death: (also SIDS, sudden infant death syndrome) death of an infant when no specific cause can be found; they seem to just stop breathing

cotinine: breakdown product of nicotine readily measured in blood, urine etc.; reliable measure of exposure to tobacco smoke

emphysema: disease of lungs in which alveoli lose elasticity; air is trapped in diseased parts of lungs, which thus can't work properly

endothelium: layer of cells lining blood vessels; controls vessel wall muscle, prevents clotting inside blood vessel; damaged by smoking

enzymes: proteins which speed up biochemical reactions although not directly involved

gangrene: death of tissues due to insufficient blood supply

germ: (pathogen) any microorganism capable of causing disease; includes bacteria, viruses, fungi, yeasts

homocysteine: an amino acid found in blood; high levels suggest a high risk of cardiovascular disease

inflammation: part of the healing response to injury or infection; affected area is red and hot (increased blood flow), swollen and tender or painful

inflammatory: causes inflammation

ischaemic heart disease: disease of heart muscle due to insufficient blood supply

keratosis: (smoker's) hard white growth of keratin (material in finger nails and hair) produced inside the mouth in response to repeated exposure to heat and tobacco smoke

larynx: voice box

leukoplakia: 'white plates', i.e. patches of keratosis

lymphocyte: white blood cell from the immune system

macrophage: 'big eater'; blood-borne repair and cleaning cell found all over the body, especially at sites of injury or infection; lungs have their own population of macrophages

macula: (in the eye) small area of retina responsible for detailed vision

mucus: clear thick liquid secreted to keep airway (and other) surfaces moist, trap dirt, germs etc.

myocardial infarct: death of a patch of heart muscle due to insufficient blood supply

nebulizer: device for producing a fine spray

neutrophil: phagocyte which specializes in killing germs

nitric oxide: NO, gas made by endothelial cells to relax blood vessel wall muscle. Also made by many other cells and used for communication between cells

nitrogen dioxide: NO_2 gas produced by burning tobacco and many other things, also by fermentation of grass to silage; highly irritant to lung tissue, producing oedema and ultimately emphysema

non-invasive: not involving inserting any physical object (needle, probe etc.) into the body

oedema: swelling caused by fluids from blood entering tissues

oxidant: causing oxidation, i.e. combination with oxygen; burning, rusting, corrosion

passive smoker: anyone, including a baby in the womb, absorbing someone else's smoke

pathogen: microorganism such as bacterium, virus, yeast, fungus, capable of causing disease

peripheral vascular disease: disease of the blood vessels supplying legs and sometimes arms; vessels are inflamed and blocked with clots; can lead to gangrene

phagocytes: cells which eat debris, old blood clots, germs etc.; part of the white cell population in blood; busy at sites of injury or infection, involved in repairs

plasma: liquid left when the cells and platelets have been removed from blood; water-based

platelets: cell fragments in blood responsible for starting clots to plug wounds

red blood cells: most of the cells in blood; carry oxygen and carbon dioxide; made in bone marrow

serum: liquid left after blood has clotted; plasma without the clotting proteins

smokeless tobacco: chewing tobacco and snuff

spasm: sudden contraction of a group of muscle cells; vasospasm, **bronchospasm:** constriction of blood vessel, bronchus

stroke: failure of blood supply (blockage, bursting) to brain tissue, causing loss of some brain function

ultrasound: sound waves of frequencies too high to be heard (higher than 30 kHz); frequencies from 1.6–10 MHz are used to produce pictures of structures inside the body

white blood cells: tiny proportion of the cells in blood: phagocytes (made in bone marrow) and lymphocytes (part of immune system; made in lymphatics)

Appendix III

References

Chapter 2

- Financial Statistics. Office for National Statistics. London: HMSO, June 1997
- Euromonitor. Market Research GB, August 1996;110–3.
- Peto R. Smoking and death: the past 40 years and the next 40. BMJ 1994;309:937–9.

Chapter 3

- Whitehead R, editor. The UK Pesticide Guide. Cambridge: University Press/CAB International/British Crop Protection Council, 1995.
- Wonnacott S, Russell MAH, Stolerman IP, editors. Nicotine Psychopharmacology. Oxford: OUP Science Publications, 1990.
- Stedman's Medical Dictionary, 26th edition. Baltimore: Williams and Wilkins, 1995.
- Gilman AG, Goodman LS, Gilman A, editors. The Pharmacological Basis of Therapeutics. New York: Macmillan, 1980.
- Richardson ML, Gangolli S, editors. The Dictionary of Substances and their Effects. Cambridge: The Royal Society of Chemistry, 1994.
- US Department of Health and Human Services. The health consequences of smoking: nicotine addiction. A report of the US Surgeon General. Washington DC: US Government Printing Office, 1988.
- Epping-Jordan MP, Watkins SS, Koob GF, Markou A. Dramatic decreases in brain reward function during nicotine withdrawal. Nature 1998;393:76–9.

Chapter 4

- Luck W, Nau H. Nicotine and cotinine concentrations in serum and urine of infants exposed via passive smoking or milk from smoking mothers. J Pediatr 1985;107:816–20.

Chapter 5 and Appendix 1

- Anderson JR, editor. Muir's Textbook of Pathology, eleventh edition. London: Edward Arnold, 1980.
- Hampton JR. Cardiovascular Disease. London: William Heinemann

Medical Books, 1983.

- Taussig MJ. Processes in Pathology. Oxford: Blackwell Scientific Publications, 1979.
- Cunningham AJ. Understanding Immunology. New York: Academic Press, 1978.
- Cawson RA, Eveson JW. Oral Pathology and Diagnosis. London: William Heinemann Medical Books, 1987.
- Gadek JE. Adverse effects of neutrophils on the lung. Am J Med 1992;92 Suppl 6A:27S–31S.
- Hunninghake GW, Crystal RG. Cigarette smoking and lung destruction. Accumulation of neutrophils in the lungs of cigarette smokers. Am Rev Respir Dis 1983;128:833–8.
- Wynder EL, Graham EA. Tobacco smoking as a possible etologic factor in bronchogenic carcinoma. JAMA 1950;143:329–36.
- Doll R, Hill AB. Smoking and carcinoma of the lung. A preliminary report. BMJ 1950;ii:739–48.
- Doll R, Peto R, Wheatly K, Gray R, Sutherland I. Mortality in relation to smoking: 40 years' observation on male British doctors. BMJ 1994;309:901–11.
- Lapp NL, Morgan WK, Zaldivar G. Airways obstruction, coal mining, and disability. Occup Environ Med 1994;51:841–2.
- Fishwick D, Fletcher AM, Pickering CA, Niven RM, Faragher EB. Respiratory symptoms and dust exposure in Lancashire cotton and man-made fibre mill operatives. Am J Respir Crit Care Med 1994;150:441–7.
- Pacht ER, Kaseki H, Mohammed JR, Cornwell DG, Davis WB. Deficiency of vitamin E in the alveolar fluid of cigarette smokers. Influence on alveolar macrophage cytotoxicity. J Clin Invest 1986;77:789–96.
- Miyamoto H, Araya Y, Ito M, Isobe H, Dosaka H, Shimizu T et al. Serum selenium and vitamin E concentrations in families of lung cancer patients. Cancer 1987;60:1159–62.
- Risch HA, Howe GR, Meera J, Burch JD, Holowaty EJ, Miller AB. Are female smokers at higher risk for lung cancer than male smokers? Am J Epidemiol 1993;138:281–93.
- Risch HA, Howe GR, Meera J, Burch JD, Holowaty EJ, Miller AB. Lung cancer risk for female smokers [letter]. Science 1994;263:1206–8.
- Zang EA, Wynder EL. Differences in lung cancer risk between men and women: examination of the evidence. J Natl Cancer Inst 1996;88:183–92.

- Cohen S, Tyrrell DAJ, Russell MAH, Jarvis MJ, Smith AP. Smoking, alcohol consumption and susceptibility to the common cold. Am J Public Health 1993;83:1277–83.
- Clayman GL, Ebihara S, Terada M, Mukai K, Goepfert H. Report of the Tenth International Symposium of the Foundation for Promotion of Cancer Research: Basic and Clinical Research in Head and Neck Cancer [meeting report]. Jpn J Clin Oncol 1997;27(5) (in press).
- Lehr HA, Frei B, Arfors KE. Vitamin C prevents cigarette smoke-induced aggregation and adhesion to endothelium in vivo. Proc Natl Acad Sci USA 1994;91:7688–92.
- Blann AD, McCollum CN. Adverse influence of cigarette smoking on the endothelium. Thromb Haemostas 1993;70(4):707–11.
- Quillen JE, Rossen JD, Oskarsson HJ, Minor RL, Lopez AG, Winniford MD. Acute effect of cigarette smoking on the coronary circulation: constriction of epicardial and resistance vessels. J Am Coll Cardiol 1993;22:642–7.
- Benowitz NL, Porchet H, Jacob P III. Pharmacokinetics, metabolism and pharmacodynamics of nicotine. In: Wonnacott S, Russell MAH, Stolerman IP, editors. Nicotine Psychopharmacology. Oxford: OUP Science Publications, 1990;112–57.
- Green MS, Juch E, Luz Y. Blood pressure in smokers and non-smokers: epidemiologic findings. Am Heart J 1986;111:932–40.
- Groppelli A, Giorgi DMA, Omboni S, Parati G, Mancia G. Persistent blood pressure increase induced by heavy smoking. J Hypertens 1992;10:495–9.
- Cole CW, Hill GB, Farzad E, Bouchard A, Moher D, Rody K et al. Cigarette smoking and peripheral arterial occlusive disease. Surgery 1993;114:753–7.
- Howard G, Wagenknecht LB, Burke GI, Diez-Roux A, Evans GW, McGovern P et al., for the Atherosclerosis Risk In Communities Investigators. Cigarette smoking and the risk of atherosclerosis. JAMA 1998;279:119–24.

Chapter 6

- Christen WG, Glynn RJ, Manson JE, Ajani UA, Buring JE. A prospective study of cigarette smoking and risk of age-related macular degeneration in men. JAMA 1996;276:1178–9.
- Silverstein P. Smoking and wound healing. Am J Med 1992;93(1A):22S–24S.
- Williams, HC. Smoking and psoriasis. BMJ 1994;308:428–9.
- Vine MF, Margolin BH, Morrison HI, Hulka BS. Cigarette smoking

and sperm density: a meta-analysis. Fertil Steril 1994;61:35–43.

● Pacifici R, Altieri I, Gandini L, Lenzi A, Pichini S, Rosa M et al. Nicotine, cotinine and trans-3-hydroxycotinine levels in seminal plasma of smokers: effects on sperm parameters. Ther Drug Monit 1993;15:358–63.

● Condra M, Morales A, Owen JA, Surridge DH, Fenemore J. Prevalence and significance of tobacco smoking in impotence. Urology 1986; 27:495–8

● Juenemann KP, Lue TF, Luo JA, Benowitz NL, Abozeid M, Tanagho EA. The effect of cigarette smoking on penile erection. J Urol 1987;138: 438–41

● Van Voorhis BJ, Dawson JD, Stovall DW, Sparks AE, Syrop CH. The effects of smoking on ovarian function and fertility during assisted reproduction cycles. Obstet Gynecol 1996;88:785–91.

● Simons AM, Phillips DH, Coleman DV. Damage to DNA in cervical epithelium related to smoking tobacco. BMJ 1993;306:1444–8.

● Pullan RD, Rhodes J, Ganesh S, Mani V, Morris JS, Williams GT et al. Transdermal nicotine for active ulcerative colitis. N Engl J Med 1994;330:811–5.

● Kellar KJ, Wonnacott S. Nicotinic cholinergic receptors in Alzheimer's disease. In: Wonnacott S, Russell MAH, Stolerman IP, editors. Nicotine Psychopharmacology. Oxford: OUP Science Publications, 1990;341–73.

● Ott A, Slooter AJ, Hofman A, van Harskamp F, Witteman JC, Van Broekhoven C et al. Smoking and risk of dementia and Alzheimer's disease in a population-based cohort study: the Rotterdam Study. Lancet 1998;351:1840–3

● Reavill C. Action of nicotine on dopamine pathways and implications for Parkinson's disease. In: Wonnacott S, Russell MAH, Stolerman IP, editors. Nicotine Psychopharmacology. Oxford: OUP Science Publications, 1990;307–40.

● Moll H. The treatment of post-encephalitic Parkinsonism by nicotine. BMJ 1926;1:1079–81.

● Ishikawa A, Miyatake T. Effects of smoking in patients with early-onset Parkinson's disease. J Neurological Sci 1993;117:28–32.

● Chiba M, Masironi R. Toxic and trace elements in tobacco and tobacco smoke. Bull WHO 1992;70(2):269–75.

Chapter 8

● Sorahan T, Lancashire RJ, Hulten MA, Peck I, Stewart AM. Childhood cancer and parental use of tobacco; deaths from 1953–1955. Br J Cancer 1997;75:134–8.

- Ji BT, Shu XO, Linet MS, Zheng W, Wacholder S, Gao YT et al. Paternal cigarette smoking and the risk of childhood cancer among offspring of non-smoking mothers. J Natl Cancer Inst 1997;89:238–44.
- Vine MF. Smoking and male reproduction: a review. Int J Androl 1996;19:323–37.
- Zenzes MT, Puy LA, Bielecki R. Immunodetection of benzo[a]pyrene adducts in ovarian cells of women exposed to cigarette smoke. Mol Hum Reprod 1998;4:159–65.
- Holmes PR, Soothill PW. Intra-uterine growth retardation. Curr Opin Obstet Gynecol 1996;8:148–54.
- Soothill PW, Morfa W, Ayida GA, Rodeck CH. Maternal smoking and fetal carboxyhaemoglobin and blood gas levels. Br J Obstet Gynecol 1996;103:78–82.
- Bardy AH, Seppälä T, Lillisunde P, Kataja JM, Koskela P, Pikkarainen J et al. Objectively measured tobacco exposure during pregnancy: neonatal effects and relation to maternal smoking. Br J Obstet Gynecol 1993;100:721–6.
- Beratis NG, Varvarigou A, Makri M, Vagenakis AG. Prolactin, growth hormone and insulin-like growth factor-1 in newborn children of smoking mothers. Clin Endocrinol 1994;40:179–85.
- Soothill PW, Ajayi RA, Campbell S, Ross EM, Nikolaides KH. Fetal oxygenation at cordocentesis, maternal smoking and childhood neuro-development. Eur J Obstet Gynecol Reprod Biol 1995;59:21–4.
- Fleming PJ, Blair PS, Bacon C, Bensley D, Smith I, Taylor E et al. Environment of infants during sleep and risks of the sudden infant death syndrome: results from 1993–5 case-control study for confidential inquiry into stillbirths and deaths in infancy. BMJ 1996;313:191–5.
- Blair PS, Fleming PJ, Bensley D, Smith I, Bacon C, Taylor E et al. Smoking and the sudden infant death syndrome: results from 1993–5 case-control study for confidential inquiry into stillbirths and deaths in infancy. BMJ 1996;313:195–8.
- Frischer T, Kühr J, Meinert R, Karmaus W, Urbanek R. Influence of maternal smoking on peak expiratory flow rate in school children. Chest 1993;104:1133–7.
- Weiss ST. Environmental tobacco smoke and asthma [editorial]. Chest 1993;104:991–2.
- van de Kamp JL, Collins AC. Prenatal nicotine alters nicotinic receptor development in the mouse brain. Pharmocol Biochem Behav 1994;47:889–900.

- He Y, Lam TH, Li LS, Li LS, Du RY, Jia GL et al. Passive smoking at work as a risk factor for coronary heart disease in Chinese women who have never smoked. BMJ 1994;308:380–384.
- United States Environmental Protection Agency. Respiratory health effects of passive smoking: lung cancer and other disorders. EPA/600/6–90/006F. December 1992.
- Wald N, Booth C, Doll R, Howard G, Jarvis M, Lane DJ et al. Passive smoking. A health hazard. Imperial Cancer Research Fund and Cancer Research Campaign 1991.
- Hackshaw AK, Law MR, Wald NJ. The accumulated evidence on lung cancer and environmental tobacco smoke. BMJ 1997;315:980–8.
- Law MR, Morris JK, Wald NJ. Environmental tobacco smoke exposure and ischaemic heart disease: an evaluation of the evidence. BMJ 1997;315:973–80.

Chapter 9

- Living in Britain 1994. General Household Survey. London: HMSO, 1994;81–93.
- Diamond A, Goddard E. Smoking among secondary school children in 1994. Office of Population Censuses and Surveys. London: HMSO, 1994.
- While D, Kelly S, Huang W, Charlton A. Cigarette advertising and the onset of smoking in children: questionnaire survey. BMJ 1996;313:398–9.
- Hastings GB, Ryan H, Teer P, MacKintosh AM. Cigarette advertising and children's smoking: why Reg was withdrawn. BMJ 1994;309:933–7.
- Roberts J. US cigarette companies attract young smokers. BMJ 1994;309:629–30.
- Klesges RC, Klesges LM. The relationship between body mass and cigarette smoking using a biochemical index of smoking exposure. Int J Obesity 1993;17:585–91.
- Shimokata H, Muller DC, Andres R. Studies in the distribution of body fat. III. Effects of cigarette smoking. JAMA 1989;261:1169–73.
- Istvan JA, Nides MA, Buist SA, Greene P, Voelker H (for the Lung Health Study Research Group). Salivary cotinine, frequency of cigarette smoking and body mass index: findings at baseline in the Lung Health Study. Am J Epidemiol 1994;139:628–36.
- Russell MAH. Nicotine intake and its control over smoking. In: Wonnacott S, Russell MAH, Stolerman IP, editors. Nicotine Psychopharmacology. Oxford: OUP Science Publications, 1990;374–418.

- Stolerman IP. Behavioural pharmacology of nicotine in animals. In: Wonnacott S, Russell MAH, Stolerman IP, editors. Nicotine Psychopharmacology. Oxford: OUP Science Publications, 1990;298–9.
- Pianezza ML, Sellers EM, Tyndale RF. Nicotine metabolism defect reduces smoking. Nature 1988;393:750.
- West R, Hajek P, Burrows S. Effect of glucose tablets on craving for cigarettes. Psychopharmacol 1990;101:555–9.
- Arciti C, Pistone M, Persici P, Gallo M, Barbieri A, Santi L. Campaigns against smoking: compliance and results. Anticancer Res 1994;14:283–8.
- Centre for Health Promotion. Effects of plain packaging on the image of tobacco products among youth. Toronto: University of Toronto, 1993.
- Charlton A, While D. Blood pressure and smoking: observations on a national cohort. Arch Dis Child 1995;73:294–7.

Chapter 10

- Ross MA, Crosley LK, Brown KM, Duthie SJ, Collins AC, Arthur JR et al. Plasma concentrations of carotenoids and antioxidant vitamins in Scottish males: influences of smoking. Eur J Clin Nutr 1995;49:861–5.
- Mawson D. Mawson's Antarctic diaries. London: Unwin Hyman Ltd, 1988.
- Shearman DJC. Vitamin A and Sir Douglas Mawson. BMJ 1978;1:283–5.
- Gilman AG, Goodman LS, Gilman A, editors. The Pharmacological Basis of Therapeutics. New York: Macmillan, 1980.

Appendix I references are included with those for Chapter 5.

Index

A

Acetaldehyde, 25, 125
Acetone, 26
Acrolein, 25, 125
Acute tolerance, 148
  cigarette, Parkinson's
  disease, 65
Addiction, 19-20, 31, 87, 90-
  91, 112
  genetic factor, 91
  pipe and cigar, 12
Advertising
  in developing countries, 21
Advertising, 18-19, 80, 116
  ban, 97, 115
  children, 19, 86, 87-89
  cross-marketing, 97
  Dave Goerlitz, 88
  in developing countries, 20
  'Reg', 88
  via sponsorship, 17
  women, 89
Advertising Standards
  Authority, 80, 88
Ageing
  arteries, 149
  brain, 63
  skin, 60
  tobacco, 9
Air or wind pipes. See Bronchi
Airway irritability, 43, 70
Alcohol and tobacco, 47, 59, 73
Alveoli, 36, 37, 41, 42, 126,
  127, 131, 133
Alzheimer's disease, 63-64
Americas, 2-3
Ammonia, 26
Amputation, 51, 145
Anaesthetist, 69-71
Aneurysm, 146
Angina, 53, 152, 153
Anti-oxidants, 99-100
Aorta, 146-47, 151
Arterial wall thickening, 81-82,
  148-49

Arteries, 141
  bursting, 146
  damaged by smoke, 143-44
  elasticity, 147
Arterioles, 141
ASH, viii, 95
Asthma, 68, 78, 120, 124, 133
Atheroma, 143, 144
Atherosclerotic plaques. See
  atheroma

B

Bangladesh, 22
Black hairy tongue, 73
Bladder, 38, 58
Blocked vessels, 48, 51, 52-53,
  144-46
  coronaries, 152, 153, 154
Blood, 53-54, 55, 138-41
  carbon monoxide, 54
  clotting, 53, 140-41
  smokers, 141
  composition, 139
  damaging endothelium, 49
  nicotine level, 90
  smokers', 139-40
  turbulent flow, 136
Blood pressure
  acute tolerance to nicotine, 54
  predictor of smoking, 97
  raised by nicotine, 148
  sky high, 69
Blood vessels, 48-52, 55, 141-49
Bombay, 47
Bone, 38, 62-63
Brazil, 20
Breast milk, 30, 34, 38, 78
British Association, 98
Bronchi, 36, 124, 125, 126, 133
Bronchiole, 36, 124, 125, 126,
  127, 131
Bronchitis, 23, 42-43, 48, 67,
  124-26
Bronchodilator drugs, 42, 132
Buerger's disease, 145

C

Cadmium, 34, 38, 76
  breast milk, 78
Cancer, 134

bladder, 58
cervical, 62
kidney, 58
liver, 59
lung. See Lung cancer
mouth, 72-73
mouth and throat, 45
oesophagus, stomach, colon,
  rectum, 58
pancreas, 59
scrotum, 61
Cancer treatment, a luxury for
  the wealthy, 47
Capillaries, 142
Carbon dioxide, 27, 37, 127,
  138
Carbon monoxide, 54, 70
  fetus, 76
  heart and, 152
  increased by filters, 27
  lethal level, 27, 54
  oxygen transport and, 27,
  140
  peripheral vascular disease,
  145
Carcinogen, 24, 33, 44, 46, 75
Cardiovascular disease, 81, 149
  numerical risks, 55
  passive smoking, 81
Chewing tobacco, 13-14, 45,
  46, 152
Childhood cancers, 75
Children, 115, 118
  anti-smoking campaigns, 96
  awareness of adverts, 97
  buying cigarettes, 16, 120
  not starting, 95-98
Children, passive smokers, 82,
  84
  cancer, 75
  cotinine, 79
  infections, 68, 79
  lead, 34
  lower educational
  achievement, 79
  nervous system development,
  77
Children, smokers, 86

blood pressure as predictor, 97
promotion, sponsorship, 17
reasons for starting, 87
Chimney sweeps, 61
China, 1, 20, 21, 81
Chlamydiae, 144
Chronic bronchitis, 126
Cigar smokers, 46
Cigarettes, 3, 10-12, 13
cost and tax, 15-16
low tar, 116
manufacture, 10
tobacco weight, 1
underage purchase, 87, 120, 121
unfiltered, 72
Cigars, 2, 3, 9, 12, 73
Cilia, 43, 125, 126
Cirrhosis of the liver, 59
Coal tar, 32
Compensation, 20
Coronary artery constriction, 152
Coronary blood flow, 52, 150-51
Coronary flow, effect of a cigarette, 151-52
Coronary vessels, 144
Cot death, 77
Cotinine, 61, 79, 91
Coughs and colds, 41, 43, 48, 123
Counterblast to Tobacco, 6
Cutting down, 93
Cytomegalovirus, 144

D
Dave Goerlitz, 88
Defibrillation, 153-54
Dentists, 45, 71-73
Developing markets, 20-21
Diet, 99-106
Diet: what to avoid, 106
Digestive system, 38, 58

E
Ectopic pregnancy, 62
Elastic
arteries, 50, 57, 141, 146

lung tissue, 41, 42, 126-27, 131
veins, 142
Elvers, 29-30
Emphysema, 23, 40-42, 48, 67, 99, 126-33
treatment, 132
Endothelium, 140
blood clotting, 48, 137
blood pressure, role in, 52
constriction of vessel wall, 50, 143
coronaries, 152-53
damaged by angry phagocytes, 49, 103
damaged by smoker's blood, 49, 137, 152
vitamin C, 103
Environmental effects of tobacco farming, 22
Enzymes, 40, 128, 129
Erection, penile, 61
European Union, 22
Exercise, 92, 106-9
Eye, 59-60

F
Fertility, 30, 61
Fetus, 34, 75, 76, 79
Fibrillation, 153-54
Filter, 12, 27
Filter-tipped cigarette, 35
Fingers (lining airways).
See Cilia
Finland, 32
Fire, 16, 22
Food for peace, 21
Formaldehyde, 25, 125
Formula 1 sponsorship, 17, 95, 97

G
Gangrene, 145
Gas-oil tar, 32
General practitioner, 67-69
Genes
Alzheimer's disease, 64
damaged ovaries, 75
damaged sperm, 75
nicotine breakdown, 91

umbilical cord, damaged, 79
Genes, damaged, and cancer, 134
Germs on hang-gliders, 43
Glucose, 92-93
Glucose and craving, 93
Government (UK), 15, 16, 17
health promotion spending, 97
income from smoking, 16
Labour, 1997, 16
Greece, 11, 22
Green tobacco sickness, 28
Gut. See Digestive system

H
Hand-rolling cigarette tobacco.
See Smoking tobacco
Hardened smokers, 68
Hardening of the arteries, 49-50, 81-82, 148-49
Health Education Authority, 88
Health risks, minimizing, 99-109
Heart, 37, 52-55, 147, 150-54
effect of nicotine, 54, 148
healthy diet, 106
Heart attack, 53, 120, 138, 144-45, 144-45
younger men, 55
Heat and cancer, 46
Heavy metals, 34, 63, 76
bone, 38
Helicobacter pylori, 58
Herbal tobaccos, 33
Homocysteine, 144
Hormones, 57
female, 62
fetal, 76
House dust mites, 78
Hydrogen cyanide, 26, 54, 145, 152
Hydrogen sulphide, 26

I
In vitro fertilization, 62, 75
India, 6, 11, 14, 20, 23, 47
Inflammation, 40, 128, 139
Ischaemic heart disease from passive smoking, 81

Italy, 22

J

James I/VI, King, 4, 6
Jamestown, 4, 5

K

Keratosis, 72
Kidney, 38, 57-58

L

Lactic acid, 153
Lead, 34, 38, 76
 brain development, 77
 breast milk, 78
Left ventricle, 150
Legal moves against
 companies, 19
Leukoplakia. *See* keratosis
Liver, 59
Low birth weight, 76
Lung, 36-37, 39-45, 125, 127-36
 vitamin E, selenium, 104
Lung cancer, 48, 134-36
 asbestos, and, 135
 avoidance, 'stupid advice', 122
 chance of cure, 44
 deaths, 23, 134
 from passive smoking, 80
 linked to smoking, 21, 43
 numerical risks, 45, 136
 vitamin E and selenium, 44,
  135
 women, 44, 135
 young smokers, 44
Lung capacity, 42
Lung function, 70
Lymphocytes, 138

M

Macrophages, 128-31, 143,
 145, 149
Macular degeneration, 59-60
Mainstream smoke, 74
Malawi, 22
Mawson, Sir Douglas, 101
Maya, 2
Menopause, 62
Mental retardation, 34
Mercury, 34
Methanol, 25
Microphages, 128

Miscarriage, 77
Mortality, worldwide from
 smoking, 23
Mouth, 36, 38, 45-48, 71-73
 heat shield, 71
 nicotine absorbed from
  alkaline smoke, 12
Mucus, 43, 124, 125, 126
Muscle in vessel walls, 147-48
Myocardial infarct, 154

N

Native Americans, 2
Neutrophils, 129-31
New World, 2-3
NHS cost of treating smokers,
 16
Niacin, 28
Nicot, Jean, 3
Nicotiana rustica, 2, 6, 7, 11
Nicotiana tabacum, 2, 5, 6, 11
Nicotine, 27-31
 absorption from mouth, 12
 acute tolerance, 54, 148
 addiction, 19-20, 31, 90
 blood levels maintained, 90,
  93
 brain, 30, 90
 breakdown products, 57
 breast milk, 38, 78
 cardiovascular effects, 52,
  54, 148
 content in tobacco, 11
 developing brain, 77
 fetus, 76
 genetic factor in breakdown,
  91
 hormone control, and, 62
 impotence, 61
 medical uses, 31
 Parkinson's disease, 65
 pesticide, 28-29
 skin, effects on, 60
 tobacco leaf, in, 28
 toxicity, 30-31
 ulcerative colitis, 63
 yield, from cigarettes, 31
Nicotine replacement, 69, 93-
 94

Nitric oxide, 49, 143, 153
Nitrogen dioxide, 26, 127
Nitroglycerin, 152
No Smoking Day, 91
North Carolina, 4, 13
Norway, advertising ban, 19

O

Oral contraceptives, 62
Oral hygiene, 71
Oriental tobacco, 6, 11
Osteoporosis, 62-63
Ovaries, 62
Oxidation, 40, 100, 131
 vitamin E in lung, 104
Oxygen, 27, 37, 51, 54, 127,
 132, 138, 152
 extraction, 52, 151
 shortage for fetus, 76
 supply, heart, 52, 151, 153
Oxygen cylinder, 42, 133

P

Pacific Rim, 17
Pakistan, 23
Pancreas, 59
Parkinson's disease, 64-66
Passive smoking, 34, 41, 43,
 74-84, 79-82, 132
 arterial thickening, 50, 81-
  82, 149
 asthma, 78
 babies, 77-78
 children, 79, 82, 149
 planning a family, 82
 unborn babies, 74-77
 father smoking, 75
 mother smoking, 75
Penis, 61
Peripheral vascular disease, 145
Phagocytes, 40, 41, 49, 51, 60,
 103, 104, 108, 128-31,
 132, 137-40
Pipe smokers, 46, 73
Pipe tobacco. *See* Smoking
 tobacco
Placenta, 76, 77
Plasma, 138, 139
Platelets, 107, 138
Positive effects of smoking?, 63

Pot-bellied with spindly legs, 89-90
Pregnancy, 75
Prolactin, 78
Prussic acid, 26
Psoriasis, 60
Pulse, 147

Q

QUIT, *viii*, 94
Quitting, 90, 91-95, 126
  aids, 91-95
  before conception, 83
  during pregnancy, 77
  effectiveness, 42, 45, 50
  fertility treatment, before, 61
  good news, 98
  help from GP, 68

R

Raleigh, Sir Walter, 4, 5, 6
Reconstructive surgery, 47
Red blood cells, 138
Reproductive systems, 61-62
Respiratory infections, 43, 123
Retail margin on cigarettes, 15
Russia, 32

S

Selenium, 105
  lung cancer, 44, 135
Serum, 138
Shanghai, 75, 81
Side-stream smoke, 74
Silo-fillers disease, 127
Skin, 38
  blood flow restricted by nicotine, 148
Skoal Bandits, 14
Smoke
  acid/alkaline, 12
  gases in, 25
  tar, 33-35
Smoke chemicals
  access to body, 37
  buildup, 38
  excretion, 38
Smoke, constituents, 24-35
Smokeless tobacco, 45
Smoker's cough, 42-43
Smoking and age, 85-86

Smoking and class, 87
Smoking machines, 34
Smoking tobacco, 12
Snuff, 2, 3, 9, 14, 45, 152
  dipping, 14, 45, 46
Spain, 3, 29
Sperm, 30, 61, 75
Sponsorship, 16-17, 18, 19, 97, 111
Sri Lanka, 14
Strokes, 48, 50, 54, 81, 138, 144, 146
Subsidies for tobacco growers, 22
Summary panel
  circulatory system, 55
  respiratory system, 48
Sweat, 38
Sweden, 14

T

Taiwan, 21
Tar, 32-35
  cigarettes, levels, 23
  lungs, 38
  mouth, 71
Tax
  China, 20
  cigarettes, 15-16
  paid in tobacco, 5
  punitive, on tobacco, 6
Teeth, 38, 71, 73
Thailand, 21
Throat, 45-47
Tobacco
  bans, 6
  cultivation, 6-7
  curing and marketing, 7-10
  harvesting, 7
  history, 1-6
  production by countries, 20
  species, 2
  varieties, 9, 11
Tobacco companies
  multi-nationals, 21-22
  UK, tax and profits, 17-18
Tokyo, 47
Turkey, 6, 11, 20

U

Ulcerative colitis, 63
Ulcers, 58
UN Food and Agriculture Organization, 22
USSR, former, 6, 11

V

Vasa vasorum, 50, 149
VAT, 15
Veins, 142
Virginia, 4, 5, 8, 13
Virginia (tobacco), 9, 10, 11
Virginia Company, 4
Virility, 61
Vitamin A, 100-103
Vitamin C, 103
Vitamin E, 103-5, 103-5, 104, 105
  blood vessel endothelium, 103
  lung cancer, 44, 135
  smokers' lungs, 104, 131
Vitamin pills, 100
Vitamins B6, B12 and folic acid, 105

W

Waist-to-hip ratio, 89-90
"We don't smoke that s---", 88
White blood cells, 138
Wood tar, 32
World Bank, 22, 23
Wound healing, 60